ISBN 978-1-330-35142-0
PIBN 10037197

This book is a reproduction of an important historical work. Forgotten Books uses
state-of-the-art technology to digitally reconstruct the work, preserving the original format
whilst repairing imperfections present in the aged copy. In rare cases, an imperfection in
the original, such as a blemish or missing page, may be replicated in our edition. We do,
however, repair the vast majority of imperfections successfully; any imperfections that
remain are intentionally left to preserve the state of such historical works.

Similar Books Are Available from
www.forgottenbooks.com

THE

RELIGION OF THE FUTURE

BY

JOHN BEATTIE CROZIER, M.B.

LONDON

C. KEGAN PAUL & CO., 1 PATERNOSTER SQUARE

1880

1928

PREFACE.

THE ESSAYS in this volume, although unlike in title, when taken together constitute a natural unity. They have all been written with one object, viz., to separate as far as possible the non-essential and transitory elements of Religion from the essential and perennial, and to give to these latter a consistent and enduring form—a form that will satisfy the feelings of the heart, while resting on the strictest inductions of science. It is no 'new religion' that I have to offer, but is the essence of the old, purified and made credible to the modern mind. Around this, which I have ventured to call the *Religion of the Future,* I hope to unite religious thinkers of all classes in a common stand against Materialism and Atheism.

In pushing forward to the goal I have had in view, I have met with theological and metaphysical subtleties, which had to be brushed aside ; with confused notions as to the limits of Scientific Thought, which limits had to be clearly and firmly defined ; and with certain errors in philosophical *method* itself, which have hitherto either been entirely overlooked, or, if recognised, have nowhere that I am aware of been prominently brought forward. These errors, which have been the source of endless fallacies in the past, and which are still very prevalent, I have endeavoured to point out.

To render a subject so wide and complex as simple as possible, I have in each essay pursued a distinct and independent train of thought. By starting from different points, and following different routes, I have sought to attain the greatest variety with the least confusion ; and have been enabled, perhaps, to cover a greater area of thought than would otherwise have been possible within the same limits. Where the different routes (like lines drawn in different directions around the circumference of a sphere) intersect, there has been some unavoidable repetition, but as these repetitions are usually the cardinal points, on which I desire more especially to fix the attention of the reader, they will not, I trust, be considered altogether superfluous.

Besides criticism and *analysis*, each essay contains a sketch of a reconstruction or *synthesis*. The same result is reached in all, but by different facts and illustrations, or by new combinations of the same facts ; and, as all the roads lead to the same goal, the general conclusions are thus greatly strengthened.

The Essays on *Carlyle* and *Emerson* find a place in this volume for two reasons. First, because the writings of these distinguished Thinkers are the best embodiments of certain aspects of the World and Man which I wish to enforce. Secondly, because among the many able and discriminating criticisms of these writers that have yet appeared, in none, as far as I am aware, has any attempt been made to show the harmony and connection of their thoughts as a whole. The hope that after some years of careful study I might be able to meet this want is my only apology for entering on ground [1] not strictly within the scope of this volume.

I have selected Mr. Spencer as the subject of the third essay, not only because he is the most profound and far-sighted of the present school of materialists, but also because he is the only one of that school who has attempted to give to Materialism a systematic philosophical basis. If I have been in any measure successful in my resolute endeavour to destroy the *foundation* of his ' System of Philosophy,' I may for the present leave to others the task of assailing the imposing and magnificent superstructure which he has erected upon it.

I regret that I have not been able to add a chapter (which I hope at some future time to undertake) on Comte, as it would have afforded me

---

[1] I allude to the sections which treat of their views of Society and Politics.

an opportunity of contrasting his views on the
World and Man with those of Mr. Spencer and
myself, and would thus have enabled me to bring
into clearer relief the controverted points which
must be settled before the form which Religion
will eventually assume can be adequately determined. The truth is, it was not until my last essay
—the essay on Emerson—was in progress that I
had, for the first time, the privilege of reading
Comte. I was struck, on the first perusal, with
many points of agreement between his views and
my own, and especially on doctrines which I fancied
I was alone, or almost alone, in holding. But from
his religious views I entirely dissented. I shall
merely indicate here two reasons for this dissent.
The first lay in his confusion of the two planes of
thought which I have sought in this volume clearly
to separate, viz., the sensuous or material, which is
the sphere of Science, and the super-sensuous or
spiritual, which is the sphere of Religion. In looking for an object of worship in the ' phenomenal,'
and finding it in ' Humanity,' he has brought Religion down to the sensuous plane, and confounded
the sphere of Duty with that of Religion. The
second cause of my divergence from Comte lay in
his inability to find any unity in Nature. In the
essay on *Herbert Spencer* I have pointed out that
by Mr. Spencer's own admission the hypothesis of
Evolution is derived from a simpler law—a law

which I myself hold, and which I have illustrated at some length in the essay on the *Constitution of the World.* All the scientific facts, therefore, which support the theory of Evolution directly support my own views, and thus I get the benefit of his facts without his materialistic basis. But while both Mr. Spencer and myself find a unity in Nature, Comte could find none. Indeed, he expressly asserts that no such unity is possible. In his hierarchy of the sciences he makes each science include the laws of all those which lie beneath it in the scale, but with certain *special* laws of its own superadded. The consequence is that he can find no *unity of plan* in Nature, and therefore can find no *unity of power* to which to refer the phenomena of the World. In short, he can find no God, and is thrown back on the *unity of Humanity* for his Religion. Comte was a consistent thinker, and his views had an intimate connection and interdependence. Had he been able to find that unity in Nature which Science has made manifest since his time, it would have entirely altered his Religion, and his views would then have been substantially the same as my own. As it is, we are separated by a gulf which nothing can bridge.

J. B. CROZIER.

St. John's Wood : *March*, 1880.

CONTENTS.

I do not intend in the present essay to enter into a detailed criticism of Carlyle's writings. His peculiarities of style and expression, his estimate of historical characters and events, his purely literary as well as social and political opinions have all been so freely canvassed that but little ground remains to be occupied. But there is one important aspect of his works which no one hitherto has attempted to represent, and which seems to me to be worthy of consideration, and that is the relationship existing among his thoughts in so far as they are parts of one harmonious whole. That some attempt of this kind should be made is the more desirable as it is not generally believed that his opinions can be reduced into a body of systematized thought. His influence is commonly attributed to his deep moral convictions and the fiery emphasis with which they are enunciated, to his intuitive sagacity and directness of insight, to his power of realization and pictorial expression.

B

But it is not generally acknowledged that his thoughts have a most vital coherence and while resting separately on the widest inductions of observation and experience are nevertheless organically connected as parts of one great living unity. Nor is this altogether a matter of surprise. His ideas are not systematically developed, but lie scattered far apart throughout his voluminous writings, are inserted in out-of-the-way places, in side remarks, sometimes in parentheses, or are gathered as the spirit of whole books. Nevertheless, if we look closely, we shall find running like a thread through his writings a vital principle which is the soul of the facts and which degrades his histories and biographies into mere illustrations. To extract this vital principle and give it firmness and stability is the object of the present essay. For the best service that criticism can render is to let us into the central thoughts of an author and to furnish us with the key which commands his whole procedure. What we want is not the discovery of this or that particular planet, but the method of Newton ; not Othello, but the consummate knowledge of life which held any number of Othellos in solution ; not the roll of beautiful jewels but the light that can shed such radiance. The 'select beauties' of an author lose much of their force and even of their beauty when torn from the parent page. Every great writer draws his principles from

an infinitely complected web of observation and experience, as a bee its honey from a thousand flowers.
These experiences we can never know, but the light
which is reflected in the handling of his subject
may enable us to read his principles. In endeavouring, with much diffidence, to give a new setting to the thoughts of one of the greatest thinkers
of modern ages, I shall consider, first, his views
of the World; secondly, of the Human Mind; and
thirdly, of Society and Government; and shall attempt to show that the whole forms a coherent body
of thought—an organic unity.

First, then, as to his views of the World. As a
preliminary to any insight into the World, Carlyle
insists on our refraining from all attempts to explain Mind. He has therefore no sympathy with
the Materialist or Metaphysician. Mind and Matter
are the most comprehensive categories in our ex
perience. They have no community of nature or
attribute. They are the poles of existence. They
cannot therefore be comprehended. The schemer
who attempts to discover perpetual motion is
baulked by a first law of physics. The materialist
who attempts to resolve Mind into a property,
product or effect of Matter, is equally baulked by
a first principle of thought. To explain an object
we must get outside of it. Archimedes promised
to lift the earth if he could find a point of support
for his lever, but the Materialist has never been

able to get outside of himself to explain himself. As the eye cannot itself see how the eye sees, so the Mind cannot know how the mind knows. The metaphysician, too, who tries to account for what are called the faculties of the mind, to show how they arise, how the complex grow out of the simple, lies under the same impossibility. Carlyle sees the hopelessness of the attempt and characterizes it with his usual force. In his essay on '*Characteristics*' he says : ' Consider it well, Metaphysics is the attempt of the mind to rise above the mind, to environ and shut in, or as we say, *comprehend* the mind. Hopeless attempt for the wisest as for the foolishest ! What strength of sinew or athletic skill will enable the stoutest athlete to fold his own body in his arms and by lifting, lift up himself? The Irish Saint swam the Channel "carrying his head in his teeth " but the feat has never been imitated.'

Again, in speaking of Diderot, he says he has long given up the idea of attempting to understand any man, even himself, and observes that ' Every man within that inconsiderable figure of his, contains a whole Spirit-Kingdom and Reflex of the All, and though to the eye but some six standard feet in size, reaches downwards and upwards, unsurveyable, fading into the region of Immensity and Eternity. Life everywhere as woven on that stupendous ever-marvellous " Loom of Time" may be said to fashion itself of a woof of light, indeed, yet on a warp of mystic darkness, only He that created it can understand it.'

He hopes the literary *Aristos* of the future will attempt to extinguish the idle habit of 'account- ing for the Moral Sense.' 'The Moral Sense, thank God, is a thing you will never " account for ; " that, if you could think of it, is the perennial Miracle of Man ; in all times, visibly connecting poor transitory Man here on this bewildered Earth with his Maker, who is Eternal in the Heavens. By no Greatest Happiness Principle, Greatest Nobleness Principle, or any Principle whatever, will you make that in the least clearer than it already is ;—forbear, I say ; or you may *darken* it away from you altogether !'

But besides this, Metaphysical Speculation is barren of fruit also. No new truth can spring from it. As a building arises from the mechanical combination of organized materials of different kinds, so knowledge arises from the vital combination of the raw materials furnished by our different faculties. By decomposing these organized faculties into imaginary homogeneous states of consciousness we can no more build up knowledge than we can build a house with pulverised wood or stone. It is as absurd as to expect to *see* better by discovering the parts played respectively by the retina and lens of the eye. It may be objected that analysis is indispensable, as in Chemistry where we first decompose that we may afterwards recombine. But there is no analogy between physical and mental analysis. For, in the first case, we arrive at atoms which, though inappreciable to the senses perhaps, have nevertheless independent existences and modes of combination ; whereas in the latter,. we arrive at states of consciousness which have no independent existence at all. To break up an organized thought into so much ego and non-ego, so much sensation and perception, is to reduce it to elements that cannot stand alone. To resolve the organized feelings of love, pride, ambition, veneration, into different modes of pleasure and pain, is to forfeit their distinctive characters, as sunlight is lost when decomposed into the seven primary colours. One metaphysician has analyzed love, and has found it to consist of certain proportions of sensuality, pride, veneration, love of approbation, of freedom &c., but these feelings when added together do not make love. The ethereal quality has escaped in the analysis, as the finest essences do when distilled, and nothing remains behind but the earthy residue. It is evident, too, that even could we show how the Human Mind has been compounded, or detect its germs in lower animals, the knowledge would avail us nothing for insight into the World. Unless we intend to look into life through the eyes of an ape, it can profit us little to know that we have developed from an ape. The fine insight is got by mounting the high peaks of thought, as we ascend to elevated ground to get sight of objects invisible from the plain. If the prospect of the landscape or the splendours of the evening sunset can only be seen from the mountain top, we do not inquire how the mountain has been upheaved. Nor need we inquire how the mind of Man has arisen, if it alone can discern the great laws of the World and the glories of created Nature.

The Mind, then, with its mystic faculties is utterly inexplicable. It is, indeed, a gleam of light hovering over a dark unfathomable sea. If we are to interpret the World we must commence by assuming the Mind as it is, and not *vice versa*. But Mind and Matter, though divided, are also united. They are separated by a chasm which no art can bridge, and yet are everywhere vitally united. It now becomes necessary to find the terms of that union. It is a main problem of philosophy. All the narrower currents of thought flow from this, as streams from a common fountain. Its practical consequences too are immense. Carlyle, with his deep intuitive sagacity, perceived this to be the indispensable preliminary to all comprehensive thinking. The answer lay around him on all sides. Like everything of wide human concern it was to be seen on every highway. Hence Goethe called

it the 'open secret.' The materialists had dis
covered that Mind was merely an attribute or pro
duct of Matter. Carlyle, on the other hand, found
that Matter existed to represent Mind—to render it
visible and body it forth. He asks : ' The thing
Visible nay the thing Imagined, the thing in any
way conceived as Visible what is it but a garment
or Clothing of the higher celestial Invisible " un-
imaginable, formless, dark with excess of bright" ? '
This doctrine makes no assumptions and, in this
respect, is unlike the materialistic one—that Mind
is the product of Matter—where it seems to be
forgotten that the thing (Mind) to be explained is
assumed in the explanation. It neither attempts
to account for Mind, nor Matter, but merely ex
presses the observed connection between them.
Let us look at a few of the facts which support it.

Take, first, our own bodies. Through them
Mind is represented to Mind. Every gesture,
every movement, has significance. The outer accompanies the inner, like the pointers on a dial-
plate. The state of the mind—its vivacity or
apathy—is expressed in the outward motions, as
the state of the heart is felt in the pulse. In the
eye alone what a world of thought and feeling is
pictured! In a man's attitude and bearing you
may read his fortunes ; in his tone and manners, his
native texture, or acquired culture. The bygone
years of trouble and pain leave their impress on

the face, as the glacial period has left its traces on the rocks.

How expressive, again, is Form! Physiognomy is true, but we are not learned enough to fully de-cipher the inscription. Among the lower animals, form and character correspond, but in Man, races and types have been so crossed and intermixed, virtues and vices, disease and passion, have been so dashed and confounded, that the correspondence is inexact and perplexing. Nevertheless, enough remains to show the intimate connection between the two. There is always some feature that more markedly than the rest bears the impress of the character. Sometimes it is the eye or brow, again it is the mouth or jaw, the nose or chin. But the important point is that we intuitively connect Form with Character—an immense fact, counterbalancing an infinitude of adverse experiences. Beauty always refers back to spiritual attributes, and from them derives its power to awe and fascinate, as de-formity does its tendency to excite aversion or dis-gust. There can be no doubt that purity of mind has a tendency to produce lines and features that are beautiful, and that nobility of soul lends the most ignoble features a ray of its own divine majesty.

But it is in Language that we have the most accurate expression of Thought. This is more especially the case when Imagination lends her aid.

The images and pictures which Language employs
are capable of expressing the most delicate and
evanescent shades of thought and feeling. They
are taken from Nature—are Nature at the first remove. Nature first expresses her own thoughts to
us, then in turn expresses ours. This power of
making her tell for us what we wish to say is a
divine hint that the Spirit of Man and the Spirit of
Nature are One. That Nature, too, is the expression
of Mind is seen in the ideas of savages and the
early nations of the world. With minds unclouded
by metaphysics, and eyes still unsubdued by the
glare of scientific nomenclature, they saw all
natural objects and phenomena as direct manifestations of spiritual powers. But we no longer see
the divineness of natural objects—the sun, fire,
man, trees, flowers and the landscape. These have
been so long used for sensuous purposes that they
have become brutalized and degraded, as Man himself becomes when he lives for low aims. We have
come to regard the sun as useful only to save gas
or fuel, fire to boil the kettle, men to carry burdens,
trees to build houses, flowers to indulge vanity,
and the landscape to fatten sheep and oxen. By
vulgar use they have lost their divine impress, as
coins their royal stamp. We have a potent instrument of expression in Music, too, which is the peculiar language of emotion, idealised and sublimated.

If we turn to the works of Man we shall find that

there, too, the Visible, the Material, is the expres- ⌐
sion of the Invisible, the Spiritual. Every institu
tion, organization or class is the embodiment of an
Idea. The Church represents the religious idea,
the State, the idea of social well-being. All the
minor associations of men for the furtherance of
any object are held together by the idea which is
their motto and vital principle. The different
classes in society, too, are each associated with a
general idea, and the individual members take
rank or precedence accordingly. Indeed, it is the
respect paid to the general idea that preserves institutions long after they have departed in practice
from their original principle. Under this ægis they
are shielded and protected, as fine names and
euphonious phrases often conceal infamy or crime.

Even a man's clothes are significant and expressive. Carlyle, speaking in a comprehensive
way, says, 'the Cut betokens Intellect and Talent, ⌐
the Colour betokens Temper and Heart.' The hierarchy of command and obedience, necessary for the
existence of society, demands that every function
should have its expressive outward symbols.
Hence the Judge, the Policeman, the Soldier have
each their distinctive costume, without which
society would lapse into confusion. It is in this
sense that Carlyle says 'Society is founded on
Cloth.' All heraldic coats-of-arms, decorations,
flags, insignia, are symbolical, as are also all rituals,

forms and ceremonies, which call up the ideas and conceptions they represent, more vividly than the unassisted imagination could do. Thus, wherever we turn, we see that the Material exists to represent the Spiritual ; Mind, to represent Matter ; the Visible, the Invisible.

Such is Carlyle's general view of the relation between Mind and Nature. It now becomes necessary to inquire what are the attributes of that Mind of which Nature is the revelation—is the expression, and symbolic representation. The wide acceptance of religious creeds by mankind proves that the essence of their teachings is in harmony with the deepest intuitions of the soul. But, in sceptical ages, that outermost stratum of the organized Human Mind known as its conscious Intelligence, demands that the harmony be made apparent to the understanding also. The religious sentiment can now only arise, when the intellect is satisfied that the Constitution of Things is in harmony with our moral and spiritual intuitions. Otherwise there is revolt and Atheism. For there is a divine element in the mind of Man that can be loyal to nothing *lower* than itself. A brute Force as the soul and centre of this World could never command the allegiance of any lofty spirit. Nor could an unjust, lying or malicious Power. Before the human mind can bow down in awe and reverence before this mysterious Universe, it must be seen to be the expression of One Mind and Will, whose attributes are Justice, Beauty, Love, Goodness and Truth. A glance at the objections of sceptics will show this to be the case. One asserts that the Universe is not the product of One Mind and Will, but is a divided sovereignty, in which some secondary hostile Power bears partial sway. Another, that it is inconceivable that Infinite Goodness could tolerate Evil when Infinite Power could have suppressed it. A third sees no Justice in this world, and has lost all hope of a better ; while a fourth alleges that Virtue, after all, is only a form of Pleasure, and Duty a modification of selfishness —a balance of motives—a mere expediency. From these objections it is evident that many contradictions must be cleared away before the Universe can be seen to be divine. Carlyle suffered from such difficulties more acutely perhaps than most men, but by force of insight, after a valiant conflict, he succeeded in overcoming them, and his victory is a possession for us all. Gifted with a deep, devout nature, his early manhood fell on a time when the beliefs that had been the life-guidance of so many generations of men, had become discredited, and were passing away. The Christian Church had come down through the centuries encumbered with such a load of Mosaic cosmogonies, medieval theologies and superstitions, that its Divine Essence was scarcely recognized. The whole was bound up together in one heterogeneous creed, belief in which was found to be impossible. Criticism had stormed and dismantled the outworks, and the citadel itself seemed in danger Science, in her lusty youth, had so maimed and perforated the huge unwieldy mass, that by many it was abandoned, and left for dead. It was not until other days had brought a deeper insight, that its spirit was seen to be still fresh and strong—young and beautiful as in its first morning. Carlyle turned away from it in despair, and sought in the wide world for that satisfaction to his soul which had been elsewhere denied him. But there, too, he could find no rest for his feet, but wandered over God's blessed earth, as over burning sands. The whole surface of Life, like a waste battle-field, was everywhere strewn with contradictions. Good and Evil, Greatness and Meanness, lay side by side in indiscriminate confusion. The sighs of the wretched and unfortunate ascended with the wailing of the disconsolate and forlorn; and Justice seemed to have taken her flight to Heaven. On all sides lawlessness appeared to reign, and above all, Time was flying fast, roaring like a whirlwind over the silent Eternity. To reunite the disjointed limbs, to educe harmony out of this stunning dissonance, seemed a hopeless task. Carlyle tells, in the *Sartor*, of the long years of anguish he endured, before he could again look up to Nature as his mother and divine But as the contradictions he had to

wrestle with are the same to-day as when he entered the arena, it may not be unprofitable to formulate them in a definite shape, and to subject them ♪
to a brief examination. A satisfactory solution of them, if possible, may well merit the attention of the thoughtful reader. They assume many forms, but may all be reduced under a few heads. ♪
1st. That the Universe is an Aggregate of conflicting forces and not a Unity. 2nd. That it has no aim, but is purposeless and indifferent. 3rd. That Duty is only a balance of Motives, and Virtue a form of Pleasure. 4th. The existence of Evil.

As a preliminary to the consideration of these objections, it is essential to remark that the Universe is everywhere made up of living forces. The impression that the Universe is dead, has probably arisen out of the popular distinction between dead and living matter. Plants and animals are spoken of as living ; stones and earth as dead and inert. But this distinction, although convenient, is not philosophical. What we call dead matter is really made up of living forces, but these forces are in a state of stable equilibrium. The living energies of steam are the same forces, set free, as are locked up in the dull inanimate ice. A concussion of sufficient power would dissipate this rocky globe into living vapour. Carlyle says 'Think you there is ♪ anything without force and utterly dead ? Even a withered leaf has forces in it and about it, else how could it rot ?' Hence Goethe was justified in calling Nature 'the Living Garment of God.'

The Universe being everywhere made up of living forces, we come now to the first great objection, viz., that these forces form an aggregate only, not a Unity. A few considerations will help to show that this is not the case. In the Human Body, for example, there is an organic connection between all the parts, so that the smallest change in any organ affects every other. No part is detached or cut off from the rest, but the same blood and nervous energy circulates through and animates the whole. This connection and interaction constitute what may be called an organic or vital unity. It is the same with the Universe. There, too, nothing is detached, but each effect strengthens or modifies every other. 'It is a mathematical fact' says Carlyle 'that the casting of this pebble from my hand alters the centre of gravity of the Universe.' The mysterious power by which the words we utter are conveyed to the minds of others and effect changes there, is true of the Universe, and is a hint of the invisible bonds that unite all things together. Besides, the Universe is constructed on one plan. This is admitted even by the materialists. In the doctrine of Evolution they hold that the same Law is everywhere present, operating alike in the formation of solar systems and in a blade of grass. But the Unity of Nature is apprehended by our Intuitions as well as by the Intellect. All things seen from a sufficient perspective and at the right angle of observation make an *identical* impression on the mind. Through the endless variety of forms the same spirit breathes. Carlyle was especially struck with this, as indeed all poetic natures are, when standing one evening at sunset on the top of one of the mountain ranges of his native land. He writes of it in this way. 'A hundred and a hundred savage peaks in the last light of day; all glowing of gold and amethyst, like giant spirits of the wilderness, there in their silence in their solitude, even as on the night Noah's deluge first dried! Beautiful, nay solemn, was the sudden aspect to the Wanderer. He gazed over these stupendous masses with wonder, almost with longing desire, never till that hour had he known Nature, that she was One, that she was his mother and Divine. And as the ruddy glow was fading into clearness in the sky ; and the sun had now departed, a murmur of Eternity and Immensity of Death and Life stole through his soul ; and he felt as if Death and Life were one, as if the earth were not dead, as if the spirit of the earth had its throne in that splendour, and his own spirit were therewith holding communion.'

On another occasion, when resting on the high table-lands in front of the mountain, watching the tempest in the distance, and seeing the storm-clouds turning into snow, he exclaims 'How thou fermentest and elaboratest in thy great fermenting vat, and laboratory of an Atmosphere, of a World O Nature—or what is Nature? Ha! why do I not name thee God? Art not thou then the "Living Garment of God"? O Heaven, is it in very deed He then that ever speaks through thee, that lives and loves in thee, that lives and loves in me?'

This poetic intuition is of more weight than a whole catalogue of merely intellectual reasons, and is the highest test of truth. It is the certificate that the poles of thought are in a line with the poles of Nature. The wave current of feeling is the surest guarantee that the electric links are all connected. We test the delicacy of a piece of humour, for example, by the way in which it affects our feelings, as we judge of wine by the way in which it affects the palate. It is the same with the perception of the finest truths. At times, when involved in a maze of bewildering details, we are made aware, by an indefinable instinct, of the presence of the subtle principle that pervades them. Though it eludes us when we attempt to seize it, we are nevertheless conscious of its existence. In some spontaneous hour, perhaps, it reveals itself to us, announcing its presence, as it opens on the mind, with a joyous burst of emotion. The value of the intuitions as an intellectual instrument is seen, too, in the way in which .they detect the presence of

error.   In reading the writings of the Materialists
we are conscious of an inward dissatisfaction.   The
facts they adduce may be sufficient, and the reason-
ing cogent and plausible, but there always remains
in the mind of the sensitive reader a residuum of
consciousness which is still unsubdued—an inner
protest.   We feel that a fallacy is lurking somewhere, although we may be unable to detect it, as
sensitive persons are conscious of the presence of
electricity in the atmosphere before it appears in
the lightning, or as we are sensible of the least
want of harmony or sympathy among our acquaint-
ances, long before it has come up into their action
or conversation.   The Universe, then, being alive
and not dead, being a Unity and not an aggregate,
must be the expression of *One* Mind and Will.

This leads us to the second objection, viz., that
the Universe has no aim or purpose, but is an indifferent machine.   This difficulty pressed heavily on
Carlyle during his long struggle with unbelief.
Speaking of his inability to believe in the Devil even,
who, in that age of scepticism, had been pulled
down with the rest, he says : ' To me the Universe
was all void of Life, of Purpose, of Volition, even of
Hostility ; it was one huge dead, immeasurable
steam-engine, rolling on in its dead indifference to
grind me limb from limb.   O ! the vast gloomy
solitary Golgotha and Mill of Death !   Why was
the living banished hither companionless, conscious ?

Why, if there is no Devil ; nay, unless the Devil is your God.' To believe that the World is a dead indifferent machine, without aim or purpose, is fatal to all spiritual life. It is one of the contradictions that lie in our path and must be removed before we can make any progress. And yet, looking merely at the surface of things, nothing strikes us more than the apparently purposeless character of life. · It seems an endless iteration and brute repetition, without advancement. Generation after generation appear on the scene, tread the same weary round, and disappear ; and we ask impatiently, For what end? Nor, looking more closely, can we discover any law regulating the fortunes of the actors themselves. The wicked seem to succeed, the good to be trodden under or cast aside.

> The good die young,
> But they whose hearts are dry as summer's dust
> Burn to their sockets.

The capriciousness of fortune characterises Life itself. The air is full of aimless shafts—pestilence and disease—flying hither and thither, but directed by no divine hand. Our life is a perpetual dodging. No sooner do we elude one danger than another is upon us. There is no apparent purpose running through this entangled web, and human life looks like the irony of mocking spirits.

·Now, all this is sufficiently obvious. Nevertheless, a deeper inspection will disclose beneath these inharmonious particulars, 'a musical perfection, a Heaven without rent or seam.' But it is essential that we should know how the facts are to be grouped and arranged. Emerson says ' He who is immersed in what concerns person or place cannot see the problem of existence.' We must bear in mind, then, that all the complex circumstances and events of life are merely the clothing of great general Laws or Tendencies—are the dress they appear in. These Laws or Tendencies may be called the soul of the facts. A few simple principles, endlessly varied and combined, make up this magnificent panorama of life. These are physical, organic, and spiritual ; and to them we must direct our attention, if we are to find the aim and purport of the World. , On an attentive consideration, then, we shall find that they all work for the Good of the Whole, that is to say, for Justice, and that the result is a gradual progress and amelioration. Nature does not work for any particular end, but for universal benefit. Take, first, the Physical forces. The solar system must be stable, before we can have any order or progress on this particular planet. Hence we have the Law of Gravitation everywhere operative, and although, by neglecting it, I may fall and injure myself, it nevertheless works for the general good. ' Shall gravitation cease till I pass by ? ' Is the heat of the sun not beneficial, because we may have had sunstroke, or steam, because

it is explosive, or fire because it may scorch
us, or water, because it may drown us? It is
the same, too, with the Organic laws. The animal passions subserve a great general end, although
they may be abused to the detriment of the individual So, too, with the Spiritual laws. All
the great spiritual faculties of Man work for the
good of the Whole, and not for the aggrandize-
ment of the individual. Benevolence, Justice, Love,
Mercy, and Truth are the indirect workings of the
First Cause for the general welfare, through the will
and consciousness of man. If we take a general
survey of Nature, where these laws are seen in their
combined action, we shall find that provision is
made for the good of the Whole, not for the exclusive benefit of any individual. Every inch of this
wide globe is packed with life, the excess of which
flows into every cranny. The very air is full of
germs. The adaptation, too, is perfect, and just that
sort of creature that can find its existence on any
spot, is placed there, whether it be plant, insect or
worm. Every scrap of material is worked up and
utilised, and the creative superintendence is everywhere busy, regulating and adjusting all with an
eye to the Whole. There are no preferences.
Nature does not pamper one plant or animal to
starve another, but even-handed justice is done to
all. Every organism is weaponed for defence as
well as for offence. There are no lotteries, but each

draws its fair share, and care is taken that all shall be provided for—plant, animal, and tree. If a race is exposed to unusual danger, it becomes more prolific; when the danger is past, its fertility declines. As the end and ideal of civil government is to give the greatest good to all, without favour to any, so in the Divine Government of the Universe, the great Laws—physical, organic, and spiritual—work impartially for the benefit of all; and he who best obeys them is most in harmony with the decrees of his Maker, and, in the great sense, alone succeeds. This working for the good of all, constitutes Justice, and is the proof that the Mind and Will of which Nature is the interpreter and representative is Just and Good.

Not only does Nature work for Justice, but provision is also made for amelioration and progress. The races that inhabited the earth during the geologic epochs, show a steady advance in type and organization. The earlier forms disappeared, and were replaced by new and higher ones. Savages and barbarians retreat before advancing civilisation, and in the course of time disappear altogether. Among civilised nations, the tendency is to advance gradually from brute force to moral and spiritual domination. Every great discovery throws the emphasis of power from a lower to a higher plane, until all things are brought under the power of Thought. Mountains and seas are annihilated, the hostile elements are subdued, and harnessed to the will of man. Carlyle says that the invention of printing will bring on democracy, and that the discovery of gunpowder will replace brute force by spiritual. And thus, through the coming ages, we may anticipate that mankind will ascend higher and higher up the slope of ' that mountain which has no summit, or whose summit is in Heaven only.'

We now come to the third objection, which leads straight to Atheism, viz., that Duty is only a form of Selfishness, and Virtue a form of pleasure. In Carlyle's youth, this doctrine was everywhere propagated by atheists and utilitarians, and is still a main doctrine of the materialists. By these men Duty was reduced to a mere enlightened Self-interest. It was for the greatest benefit of the greatest number. You counted the cost of dishonesty, and the cost of Duty, and on the whole, Duty was found to be the more profitable. It was the best policy. It was no Divine Idea implanted in the heart of Man by his Maker, but was merely a form of selfishness, a matter of expediency. The metaphysicians had analysed it carefully, and had found it to consist of certain proportions of self-interest, force of public opinion, and love of esteem. They had ground all that was Divine out of it, and only the husks of Pleasure and Self-interest remained behind. Against this doctrine, Carlyle hurled a most indignant protest. He clearly perceived that in the heart of Man, Virtue still existed, and pointed it out. It was the inner command, 'Work thou in Well-Doing.' Men may differ as to what their special duties are, under certain circumstances, and from the confusion and uncertainty thence arising, may be tempted to doubt whether Duty itself exists, but the impulse to Well-Doing, innate and eternal, cannot·be got rid of. All men feel it, and no vulgar success, of money or fame, can entirely obliterate our consciousness of it. 'The true God's voice, voice of the eternal, is in the heart of every man—there, wherever else it be.' What each shall consider as well-doing, will depend on education and circumstances. Some think it consists in developing and extending trade and commerce ; others in cheapening the loaf, or feeding the poor. Some believe in helping others directly, others, in helping them to help themselves. There are those again, who slight these material benefits, considering them as of less importance than instructing the mind, or reclaiming the heathen and drunkard, the prostitute and slave. But in every human soul the impulse to well-doing exists. And what are all these, but more or less enlightened ideas as to how best promote, what each considers as the highest Good ? That Virtue is not a mere form of Pleasure or Self-interest, is seen also in this, that where the belief is genuine, it is attended with a self-sacrifice, grand in proportion to the purity, depth and in-

tensity of the conviction. For it, men freely give
their time, their money, their comfort, their reputation, their position, their dignity, and even life itself.
To doubt this, is rank and hopeless atheism. Carlyle
calls it 'the infinite nature of Duty,' for it has an
unlimited character in our thoughts. No metaphysical or materialistic hocus-pocus can decompose
or dissipate this primary intuition of the mind.

But while Duty, as a spiritual impulse, is eternal
and divine, the special duties of nations or individuals depend on circumstances. They must
adapt themselves to the necessities of the hour.
At one time, we must think, at another, act; now
we must fight, and again, we must pray. And
rightly so, for the world is in constant evolution and
metamorphosis, and what was yesterday a furtherance, becomes an obstruction to-day. We must
discern the tendencies of the time, throw ourselves
at their point, clear the way for them, and allow
them to act. Nature gives us the hint. Her
grand geological epochs, once completed, never
return. The old megatheria and ichthyosaura
sleep in their fossil beds, never to awake. They were
there and wanted, in their time and place, but their
age is past, and the new hour brings a new require-
ment. And as the realities and duties of life
differ in different ages, so must the spiritual
symbols that represent them. To drag some old
forgotten mummy from its grave, and insist on its

being our duty to warm it into life, is to mistake the aim and purport of this world.

This brings us to the last great contradiction of life--the existence of Evil. This has been the cause of more scepticism, perhaps, than any of the contradictions which Life presents. It has thrown its gigantic shade over our moral and spiritual life, blighting it like a poisonous tree. The seed from which it has grown, is the dogma of the *absolute* Infinitude of God. It is asked, why an omnipotent God should permit Evil, why happiness should not be the lot of us all. From a Creator *infinite* in Power and Goodness, we should expect a world free from frailty and misery. And it must be confessed that if the premises are sound, the conclusion is just and rational. But I dispute the premises. I doubt the omnipotence. And yet it has come down to us through so many centuries, consecrated by such a weight of authority, that its denial will cause a recoil of feeling in the best minds. Nevertheless, on severe examination, you will look in vain for any evidence to support it. What reason have we for believing the Creator to be *absolutely* Infinite, *absolutely* Omnipotent ? All reason points the other way. There is every reason for believing the Universe to be of *no known* limits, none for believing it to be absolutely unlimited or Infinite ; and it is a capital point in philosophy, that the burden of proof lies with the theory least in

harmony with the consolidated experience of man
kind.   All Nature points to the continued opera-
tion of a vast, but limited Power.   It is not at' all
essential to our spiritual welfare that the Creator
should be Infinite, but only that He should be
commensurate in .Power and Glory with his created
works.

From this point of view, then, the existence of
Evil is a matter of course.   It is a necessary result
of limitation.   The soul of man is boundless in its
desires and aspirations, but the poor Earth is
limited.   With many to satisfy and but little to
divide, Evil commences.   Carlyle asks if all the
finance-ministers and confectioners of Europe
would undertake to make even one shoeblack
happy, and concludes that if half a Universe were
allotted to him, he would commence quarrelling
with the proprietor of the other half, and think
himself the most ill-treated of men.

Having cleared away the superficial contradic--
tions which Life is constantly forcing on our
attention, we find our moral and spiritual intui
tions once more in harmony with the constitution
of Things.   The darkening clouds of doubt that
had drifted over the heavens, break and clear away,
and we look into the serenity of the eternal sky.
Our hearts, infolded by the cold touch of scepticism, open up again to the glory of life, like flowers
to the morning sun, and are refreshed as with dew.

We may pass, then, at once to Carlyle's Religion, which has a living organic connexion with his insight into the World. 'For Philosophy, in its true sense, is or should be the soul, of which Religion, Worship is the body.'

We have seen that the World is the product of One Mind and Will which works everywhere for Justice, Goodness, Beauty and Truth, but under conditions and limitations. From this will follow our Religion, i.e., our attitude of mind and heart towards this Supreme Being, and our practical duties in this world. The end of Nature is Justice, Goodness, Spirituality and Beauty. The immense variety of objects which make up the world of Nature, by their action and interaction work out that end. Although each of these objects has a distinct, separate existence—mineral, worm, insect, flower, tree, animal and man—they are all kept subordinate to their great end, by subtle links which attach them to the Will at the centre. Man, equally with the humblest and meanest of created things, is an instrument for working out that Justice and Beneficence which Nature has at heart. He forms part of those great world-forces that ply their unwearied spindles around him, weaving in the garment of existence. He cannot be isolated from them. He appears to enjoy an independent existence and to follow his own private ends, but he is as dependent on the Will of God, as a tree

on its mother earth. He cannot live for selfish
ness alone. He may be fanned by the sweet
breezes of pleasure, and bask in the world's bright
sunshine, but unless he is nourished through the
roots of his being which are fed from that central
Fountain, he withers away. And as the central
Law of the World is Justice and Goodness, of
which the thousandfold complexities of Physical
and Organic Law are instruments, so the central
Law of Man is *dependence* on that just and good
Will ; all the superficial laws of his nature, physical and organic, being merely instruments of this
central Law—subsidiary and subordinate to it.
Hence the first Duty of Man is Self-Renunciation.
This is a total change of heart and will, or in other
words, a conversion. It is what is known in Scripture as a being 'born again.' It is a change in the
motive-springs of action. In our natural state, our
main desire is to secure for ourselves personal
happiness, but in this, it is to do the will of God
—even at the expense of our personal happiness.
We wish God's will to prevail, even although we
should suffer. This temper of mind is mystic in its
nature, cannot be compelled, but dawns on the heart
like love. It arises when we have come to realize
that the World has been created by God for just
and good ends, and that we are His instruments.
It is not enough that we should apprehend this
merely as an intellectual truth. It must lay hold

of our hearts and sink into the soul. But it arises more readily when we see that the great and beneficent Power that controls all things, Himself works under limitations. Nor is this surprising. The parent who, possessing the power to make his child happy, should wantonly decree its misery, might command its obedience, but not its love. In the same way, no power in the Universe could prevent the free spirit of Man from rebelling against a God, who had withheld a good which he could have conferred, or permitted an evil which he could have withheld. And in the current theologies where this doctrine is avowed, it has given rise in the loftiest minds, as we all know, to a Byronic gloominess of temper and sourness of heart, in spite of the immense prodigality of agencies everywhere at work for the good of Man. But, on the other hand, when we see that the vast and beneficent Power which Nature reveals to us, Himself works under difficulties and limitations; when we see that the poor Earth has nothing more to give—'is our needy mother and not our cruel step-dame'—there rises from our hearts a burst of grateful emotion, and with loving resignation we can look up and say ' Thy will be done.' As the poor mother, who divides her last poor crust equally among her famishing children, gets their blessing, although they are still wretched and unhappy, so we mortals, miserable and heavy-

laden, seeing that the good God has, by His impart-
tial laws, fairly divided among us what He had to
give, can still bless Him, and be blessed in return.
This doctrine of Self-Renunciation is distinctive of
Christianity, and is a direct deduction from our insight into the World. It is the beginning and end
of Carlyle's religion. He constantly quotes Goethe's
remark, that 'only with Renunciation can Life be
properly said to begin' and everywhere inculcates
it as our first and highest duty. He says 'It has
ever been held the highest wisdom for a man not
merely to submit to Necessity—Necessity will
make him submit—but to know and believe well
that the stern thing which Necessity had ordered
was the wisest, the best, the thing wanted there.
To cease his frantic pretension of scanning this
great God's World in his small fraction of a brain ;
to know that it *had* verily, though deep beyond his
soundings, a Just Law, that the Soul of it was Good ;
that his part in it was to conform to the Law of
the Whole, and in devout silence follow that ; not
questioning it, obeying it as unquestionable. I say,
this is yet the only true morality known. A man
is right and invincible, virtuous and on the road towards sure conquest, precisely while he joins himself to that great deep Law of the World, in spite
of all superficial Laws, temporary appearances,
profit-and-loss calculations ; he is victorious while
he co-operates with that great central Law, not

victorious otherwise—and surely his first chance of
co-operating with it, or getting into the course of
it, is to know with his whole soul that it *is* ; that it
is good, and alone good.' Throughout his biogra
phies the great doctrine is everywhere enforced
that Manhood begins when we submit to Necessity
—when we brighten the ring of Necessity into a
ring of Duty.

The belief that Self-Renunciation is the highest
moral act is justified by the feeling which attends
it. It is a feeling of Blessedness as distinguished
from all lower forms of Pleasure, however refined.
It communicates to the soul a sense of unbounded
strength and freedom. It has upheld the saint in
the dungeon, the martyr at the stake. It was present with Him who 'trod the wine-press alone,'
an all-sustaining spirit by His side. It is the
highest emotion of which Man is capable, and is
the direct influx of the Divine. 'Feel it in thy
heart,' says Carlyle, 'and then say whether it is of
God.'

The next Duty that flows directly from a just
insight into the genius of Nature is 'to love our
neighbour.' Indeed, it is more correct to say that
it arises simultaneously with the act of Renunciation.
All contentions among men, with their concomitant misery, folly and sin, spring from the limitations which we have just been considering. With
insatiable desires, and but limited means of grati-

fying them, selfishness begins. Crammed together
in a narrow space each one struggling, 'like an
Egyptian pitcher of tamed vipers to get his *head
above* the others,' what can result but heartburnings
and hatred ? But when we have renounced our
selfishness, and conformed our wills to the Will of
God, the barriers that formerly divided us from our
fellow-men fall away, and our hearts mingle as the
waters. Carlyle says in this connection ' Man with
his so mad wants and mean Endeavours had become
dearer to me, and even for his sufferings and his
sins I now first named him Brother.' When we
have learned that no thread in this vast web of
existence is detached, but each is connected with·
all others—the poor earth, the very worm, and Man
himself—and that all are instruments in the hands
of God, all ' furtherances of what is holy,' what is
there that we cannot reverence and love ?

The Love of God and of our Neighbour are, then,
the first duties of Man. They constitute the tem
per of mind and heart which it becomes us to bear
towards our Maker and the world around us. But
the circuit of human duties is incomplete without
Action. Our principles must be converted into Con
duct. Thought and Action—these are the two
poles between which our being swings. To be
complete, each must be supplemented by the other.
Our first duty being submission to the will of God,
our second duty is to assist it by Action. ' All that

is right,' says Carlyle ' includes itself in this of
co-operating with the real Tendency of the World.'
All right action consists in obeying the Laws of
Nature, as in these God has indicated His will.
The whole will of God, so far as we are concerned,
is embodied in the whole of these Laws. Our whole
Duty, therefore, is to conform to the whole of
them. But they are an organised code, with gradation and subordination. The head of all is that
great central Law of Justice, Goodness, and Truth ·
of which all others are the subordinate instruments. Our whole duty therefore is, first, Spiritual
Obedience or Renunciation ; then, obedience to
the rest, in as far as they are consistent with this
great central Law. For example, we should avoid
fire, but if our Duty calls we must go even if
through fire. This vital union of all in one grand
obedience forms the highest type of character and
culture. It is Beauty of Character—not Asceticism,
but a noble universal manhood. This identifica-
tion of Religion with Work is everywhere insisted
on by Carlyle. He says ' Properly speaking, all
true Work is Religion ; and whatever Religion is
not Work may go and dwell among the Brahmins,
Antinomians, Spinning Dervishes or where it will ;
with me it shall have no harbour.' And again
' The essence and outcome of all religions, creeds
and liturgies whatsoever is To do one's work in a
faithful manner. What is the use of orthodoxy, if

with every stroke of your hammer you are breaking all the Ten Commandments.' We must first
study to know the Laws of God, then work to propagate them. With all men at their tasks, each
working humbly 'ever in his great Taskmaster's
eye,' what a new divine face would be put on this
old selfish world !

Self-Renunciation, Love of our Neighbour and
Work, all of which are strictly deducible from a
just insight into the World, are the main elements
of Carlyle's religion. They are also the *soul* of
the Christian religion, without its corruptions—its
excrescences, theological superadditions, metaphysical subtleties and vain sectarian refinements. To
these corruptions the prevailing scepticism is due,
almost as much as to the doctrines of scientific
Materialism. They have become so identified with
Christianity, in the vulgar mind, that denial of the
one involves that of the other. It is not difficult
to foresee that, as long as these continue, scepticism
will prevail and the influence of the Church be
seriously impaired. Is it not painful and melancholy to witness the reluctance with which these
old worn-out garments are cast aside ? Like frost-
bitten fruit shaken by the winter's wind, I see
them still clinging to the tree, long after their time
is past and their fellows have all departed. At
last they fall unnoticed, and the good earth receives
them again into her bosom. They drop silently

one by one, but sooner or later all must go, and Science does a good and even sacred work in gently hastening their fall. It has often been said, and with truth, that true Religion has nothing to fear from Science. Science deals with the physical and organic laws of Nature, which are the subordinate instruments of that central Law of Goodness, Justice and Truth, for which the World exists. She must therefore be subordinate to those Spiritual Laws of man which correspond to that central Law of the World, as the means are subordinate to the end. In her legitimate sphere she has a noble and imperative duty to perform. But she must work under the inspiration of the great truths of Religion, as a mason under an architect. And when the Christian Church has, once for all, thrown off her old rags, and rehabilitated herself in the simple garments of Renunciation, Brotherly Love, and Noble Work, she will draw to her side the great and good of all succeeding ages, and will stand on a rock, eternal and immutable, against which 'the gates of Hell cannot prevail.'

We come now to the second division of our subject viz., Carlyle's mode of representing the Human Mind. In a former part of this essay we saw that he regarded all the attempts of metaphysicians to explain or account for the Mind, as impotent and vain. We have now to remark that he equally regards their mode of representing it as.

superficial and inadequate.   Indeed, it is now
generally admitted that they have failed in their
map of the mind.   They have split it into what are
called faculties ; have thrown these faculties into
certain categories, founded on their superficial resemblances ; but have entirely overlooked the deep
connexions that bind the whole together as members of one living unity.   They have treated separately of the Intellect, of the Imagination, of the
Fancy, of the Æsthetic faculties and Moral Sentiments, as if each were independent of the rest in its
manifestations and modes of activity.   But while
these divisions are convenient for purposes of expression, they are as far from representing the
actual operations of the Mind, as a descriptive
catalogue of the organs of the body is from representing their vital play and interaction.   Of course,
there are all degrees of superficiality in these
systems, from the crude incoherent chart of the
phrenologists up to the subtle and immaterial representations of the German philosophers.   But
all, at bottom, end in analysis—in the divorce of
the faculties—whereas the problem of philosophy
is to find how they are united.   The ingenuity and
subtlety of many of these systems has imposed on
the world for profundity.   But ingenuity and subtlety are not depth of insight, but in many cases
are the reverse.   All deep thoughts are characterised by their simplicity, and although couched

in philosophic language, are at last in harmony
with the unconscious instincts of men. They are
at one with our deepest intuitions, even when at
variance with our superficial opinions. But the
metaphysician's theorem, the more it is elaborated
the more it recedes from those cardinal intuitions
which are common to humanity, and to which all
philosophy should approximate. The intuitions
of Man make an eternal and insuperable distinction between God and Force, Right and Wrong,
Duty and Pleasure; but the metaphysicians will
undertake to show that Unselfishness is really only
a form of Selfishness, Duty a form of Pleasure,
and God a form of Force. The truth is, the metaphysician proper resembles very much the perpe-
tual-motion schemer before alluded to, who, the
more he exercises his ingenuity, the more displays
his want of sight, and while constructing his most
ingenious contrivance is blind to the first laws of
physics. His intellect is of much the same type as
that of the mathematician, who deals with symbols
which have as little to do with the facts of life as
figures on a chess-board; or of the logician, whose
work can be equally well done by a machine, where
you put the premises in at one end and the conclusion
is ground out at the other. There is a long road
to travel between the insight of such men and that
of Emerson and Carlyle. And is it not a curious
fact that those who are universally admitted to

have had the profoundest insight into the human mind—Shakspeare, Bacon, Goethe—were not metaphysicians at all? They drew their wisdom from Nature at all points, lying close to her and sucking her nourishment, like the polypus, through every pore, while the metaphysician sits high aloft in the midst of his abstractions, spinning his web from his own consciousness.

If we turn from the metaphysicians to Carlyle, a broad contrast at once strikes us. Instead of ingenuity and subtlety, we have breadth and simplicity; instead of dead dismemberment, we have a living Unity. We have seen that the World is the product of One Mind and Will, which works everywhere for Justice, Beauty, Truth, and Goodness, and that to these high ends all things in Nature conspire. Each individual must, therefore, have some provision made for its own self-preservation. For this purpose Nature has furnished her creatures with certain animal propensities and physical powers—horns, claws, hoofs, fangs and stings. Properly speaking, these are not part of that Spirit that works everywhere for Justice. They are merely instruments of it. One race of animals, for example, is weaponed to exterminate another. But that other is also furnished with means of defence or escape from the first, and so the balance is preserved. This balance is Justice; but the organs of defence and offence are merely the means by which it is accomplished. Thus it is in Nature. Now, Man is the epitome of Nature, and gathers all her powers into himself. He is Nature distilled and condensed. The physiologists tell us that the human fœtus in its development from the germ, passes successively through the forms of fish, reptile, and mammal. It certainly seems as if every existence had left some hint of its nature in the mind of Man. There are threads of relation running out from Man to all things, and these are the media by which he converses with them. Accordingly we find that the same Mind, Soul, Spirit, Essence or whatever you choose to call it, which works everywhere throughout Nature, diffused over areas of brute *unconscious* life, has concentrated itself in Man and become a *conscious* existence. Its sides are, as I have said, Beauty, Justice, Goodness, &c. which are the ends of Man as they are of Nature. But like every other being, Man has an individual self which must be protected. For this purpose he, too, is equipped with certain organised powers, physical and mental. The physical comprise, besides his bodily advantages, the tools and weapons which his ingenuity devises for his self-protection, and which correspond to the horns, fangs, and jaws of the lower creation. The mental assume various forms, as Love of Life, Love of Approbation, Combativeness, Envy, Pride, Fear, which are all modes of selfishness, more or less refined, as their object is, in the widest sense, his own preservation. Now, these mental attributes, although known through the Mind, are not properly parts of the Mind, but are merely the mental instruments of Self-Preservation. Or say, rather, that although connected with the Mind, they are not parts of it. And now, observe, how this distinction is recognised by the spontaneous intuitions of mankind. When we say that a man is selfish, bigoted, vain-glorious, cowardly, false, or spiteful, we really mean that he is *wanting* in the attributes of the soul known as generosity, sympathy, humility, heroism, uprightness, or magnanimity. The one set of attributes are positive and real, like light and heat, the other negative, like cold and darkness.

If we turn to Carlyle, we shall find that he everywhere recognises this broad distinction. 'Crabbedness, pride, obstinacy, affectation,' says he 'are at bottom *want* of strength.' 'All faults are properly *shortcomings*; crimes themselves are nothing other than a *not doing enough*; a fighting but with defective vigour.' In another place he says ' The Dead are all holy to us, even they that were base and wicked when alive. Their baseness and wickedness was not *They*, was but the heavy and unmanageable Environment that lay round them, with which they fought unprevailing; *they* (the ethereal god-given Force that dwelt in them, and was their *Self*) have now shuffled off that heavy Environment, and are free and pure, &c.' Accordingly we find him everywhere ranking virtues or vices according to the degree in which they are admixed with the primary attributes of the soul, as alloyed metals are valued in proportion to the gold they contain. Speaking of the French at the time of the Revolution, he says 'Noble sentiment—the film-shadow of a raw material of Virtue, not woven, nor likely to be, into Duty—thou art better than nothing, and also worse.' In describing the 'feast of pikes' in the Champ de Mars, when the King and People, before the whole world, plighted their mutual faith, so soon alas! to be broken, he observes that 'the theatricality of a people goes in a compound ratio—ratio indeed of their trustfulness, sociability, fervency, but then also of their excitability, porosity, not *continent*; or say, of their explosiveness, hotflashing, but which does not last.' He has no sympathy with the softer emotions of our nature, unless they spring from, or rest upon, the grand attributes of the soul. 'That pity which does not rest on Justice is maudlin laxity of heart, grounded on blinkard dimness of head—contemptible as a drunkard's tears.' 'Some readers know that softness without rigour—rigour as of adamant to rest upon—is but sloth and cowardly baseness, that without Justice first, real pity is not possible, and only false pity and maudlin weakness is possible. Others again are not aware of that fact.' The Exeter Hall philanthropy, that claims fraternity with criminals, and builds model prisons for their accommodation and comfort, he denounces as an 'indiscriminate mashing-up of Right and Wrong into a patent treacle,' and predicts that ' it will one day be drummed out of the world, with due placard stuck on its back, and the populace flinging dead cats at it.' He speaks of the good Howard in mildly contemptuous terms, and admits that his regard for him lies a long way on this side of idolatry. The smooth-shaven cleanness that, with its fine phrases and sentiments, simulates Virtue, but behind which there is no heart, is his special abomination. It is Insincerity, the parent of Cant religions, Cant moral, Cant political. On the other hand, his heroes have all the primary virtues of sincerity, veracity, insight—Cromwell, Frederick the Great, Johnson, Burns, Luther, Shakspeare. The high premium he sets on these attributes explains his love for such strong and even brutal characters as Frederick William and William the Conqueror. He will forgive or palliate anything in a man— crimes like Danton's, excesses like Mirabeau's— provided he can show him a general superabundance of heart and soul. He admires the savage bloody valour of the Norsemen, and their superiority to fear ; and considers that the extent to which we have put fear under our feet is, even now, a good measure of manhood.

With this broad division of the Mind into the attributes of Mind proper, or soul, and the attributes pertaining to Man as an individual, (the latter being merely negative, the former alone being positive and real), we may now pass to Carlyle's great Law of the Unity of the Mind. The attributes of the Soul are Justice, Goodness, Beauty, Truth, Magnanimity, Sincerity, Valour, Mercy, Reverence &c. These are its different sides, different affections of the mind in which it is present. It breaks itself into these different forms according to the side of the mind on which it acts, as light is broken into different colours according to the nature of the object on which it falls. Now, there can be no doubt that individuals differ immensely in their susceptibility or openness to these different affections of the mind. The poet lies more open to the Divine currents on the side of Beauty, the moralist and saint on the side of Justice and Reverence, the philosopher on the side of Truth, the heroic heart on the side of Valour and Magnanimity. Nor is the difference one in kind only. It is also in quality and degree. These differences depend on Temperament, or the way in which the general Soul incorporates itself with the organization of the individual. But just as in physics, the movements of bodies in relation to each other are not chaotic, but follow fixed laws,

so the superficial movements of the mind obey a
profounder law—the law of Unity.   This law may
be defined to be—the tendency which the excitation
of any one attribute of the soul has to excite the
rest, to arouse not one virtue merely, but all.   We
are all conscious of this, at times.   When the flood-
gates of the mind open up to the entrance of the
Soul, under the inspiration of music or of a tale of
heroism, we are conscious of more Magnanimity,
more Justice, more Pity, more Sincerity, more
Resignation.   In some men such states of mind
are habitual, and their life takes its impress from
them, but in most they are occasional only ; the
individual relapsing into his ordinary routine.
But it is in these high moments that we catch
sight of the Law of Unity, as we catch sight of the
laws of Electricity, for example, when we get it
concentrated.   We may see this law, too, in our
experiences of men.   The man who stands for a
great principle and is ready to sacrifice himself for
it, blossoms into all the virtues.   But the virtue
displayed must be a true virtue, springing from the
character, not a mere patchwork overlaid on it, or
the result of custom merely.   Politeness, as we all
know, may go with heartlessness, church-going
with irreligion, almsgiving with vanity.   Honour
may co-exist with dishonesty.   But when a man
has renounced himself and become the servant of
God, it is quite certain that all the virtues spring up

in his heart—sincerity, justice, patience, courage, reverence, and resignation. Perhaps there is no doctrine that Carlyle impresses more frequently, and with greater emphasis, on his readers than this. He says the just man is, at bottom, the good man, the merciful man. When rough old Johnson finds a poor wretched prostitute fallen on the streets and carries her home on his shoulders ;—when Balder the Sun-God of the Norse mythology, sends his ring to Odin, and his wife sends her thimble to Frigga as a remembrance, Carlyle remarks that ‘true Valour is the fountain of true Pity also.’ He will allow of no separate virtues, but, as the same light shines through them all, they must be all convertible. ‘Justice is only another form of the Reality we love.’ The hero is not distinguished from other men by any high transcendental or exceptional quality, but merely by the simple virtue of Sincerity. Religion itself he considers to be only another form of the same virtues. Frederick the Great, who flirted with French Scepticism, nevertheless ‘showed his religion by his veracity and respect for facts,’ and Abbot Sampson by ‘doing his duty faithfully in *this* world, where his work lay awaiting him.’ He defines Worship to be ‘transcendent Admiration’ The love of Nature, that inspires the true poet and artist, he regards as a kind of diluted worship, whilst ‘Beauty in its highest clearness is religion.’ The Beautiful and

the Good have the same connection and converti-
bility. One great writer says that 'the sound-
ness of the bone ultimates itself in the peach-bloom
complexion ;' and Carlyle echoes Goethe's saying
that the 'Beautiful includes the Good.'

We are now in a position to consider the most
important aspect of this doctrine of the Unity, viz.
that the Intellectual and Moral faculties are One,
—are but different sides of the same indivisible
Unity—a living Mind. This doctrine has been
very much questioned and I find as yet but little
recognition of it in contemporary thought. But I
venture to regard it as one of the profoundest in
philosophy, and more fruitful perhaps than any
other. It was a favourite topic of dispute between
Carlyle and his friend Sterling. Carlyle affirmed
that the Intellect was not a separate faculty, but
the result of the union of all the faculties ; and that
between the Intellectual and the Moral or Spiritual
there was, in all cases, the strictest correspondence.
Sterling, on the other hand, contended that the
Intellectual faculties might be deep and comprehensive where the Moral were weak ; and in his
essay on 'Carlyle' adduced, among other things, a
number of historical examples to support it. And
as this opinion is one that is very widely held, it
may be well to devote a short space to its consideration. The indispensable condition to a just intellectual perception of a thing, is to have a true

image or mental representation of that thing. And as the eyesight is common to us all, the difference between one man and another must depend on what the eye is stimulated to see. This stimulus must come from the other attributes of the mind— its width of sympathy, its intensity, its fineness and sensibility. In the ordinary intellectual perception of the man of business or politician, we may see how the vision is sharpened by self and party interest. But when we come to the realm of Intellect proper—to the higher and wider vision of the Poet and Philosopher—the dependence of the intellectual on the moral and spiritual is still more intimate. The poetic Thinker's representation of Life, his insight into the World and Man, comes directly from his openness of mind and power of sympathy, that is to say, from the depth, fineness, and intensity of his moral nature. To begin with, he must have had *love* and *reverence*, to put himself into the proper attitude for reception ; he must have had *sympathy*, to catch the spirit of things ; *sincerity*, *patience*, and *humility*, to see them dispassionately in spite of obstruction and difficulty ; *magnanimity*, to resist the bigotry, prejudice, and pressure of surrounding opinion ; *justice*, to adhere to the right and true in spite of the shock to his most cherished convictions. Now, these are all moral and spiritual attributes, and are inseparable from any profound insight into Life. Indeed,

I know of no author who has attained to real depth
and comprehensiveness, in whom these virtues are
not apparent. There is a general elevation of
mind,—a general openness to great thoughts and
emotions—shining through the pages of great
writers, which is the light that has illumined their
intellects. Where this temper of mind is wanting
there may be ingenuity, subtlety, wit, rhetoric,
logic, but never depth or originality. I am, of
course, aware of those special aptitudes which are
made so much of at schools and colleges, as quick-
ness, power of memory, calculation and the like.
These are the results of temperament or fortunate
constitution, often of some overgrown cell in the
brain, but have little appreciable influence on the intellectual power. Great feats of memory or calculation, great facility in learning languages or music,
do not, either alone or in combination, constitute a
great intellect. Indeed, instances might be quoted,
in abundance, where these powers have been ab-
normally developed, and yet have coexisted with
an almost total want of human insight, and even
with idiocy. But the fact is, the identity of our
moral and *intellectual* nature cannot be made
apparent by any enumeration of examples, but by
a careful observation of the relations subsisting between them in our own minds. We shall find that
the finer and deeper secrets of any art disclose
themselves to those only who love it for its own

sake ; that they remain hidden to those who culti-
vate it for money or applause, and only those
superficial aspects of it which are marketable or
'practical' will be seen. It is true that men of eminent
talents have sometimes turned them into a marketable commodity. But, if we consider it, they must at
one time have loved their art and cultivated it for
itself alone, or they never would have attained their
mastery over it. We shall find, too, that, if, on
any subject, we have a point of prejudice, of pride,
of bigotry, or obstinacy, our knowledge on that subject will be less exact, deep, and comprehensive ; as
it will also be, in proportion as our egoism, affectation, insincerity, interpose between our mind and
the object we are endeavouring to represent, ob-
scuring or distorting the image. Is a man dull or
unimpressionable on any side of his mind, lacking
in sympathy with any side of Nature or Life ?
Then that side will remain dark and unknown to
him. If his sympathies generally are dull, he may
be a metaphysician, logician, senior-wrangler or
double-first, but not a great Thinker. Is his mind
dead to the great mystery of existence, to the
nature of the Universe, and his duties and destiny
in it, caring only for it in as far as it is a good
kitchen garden ? Then he will lack breadth of
thought, elevation of mind, and all that constitutes
greatness. Does he look at life with the eye of a
diplomatist, an attorney, or a detective ? Then he

will see only the weaknesses of men—their idio-
syncrasies, their vices, their infirmities of temper or
will—but the nature of Man he will never see.
Carlyle calls this stamp of intellect 'the *vulpine*
intellect which knows where the geese lodge,' and
asks contemptuously, 'what else does it know than
this or the like of this'? Beecher compares men
of this class to cats that sit watching the rat-holes
of life, and let the elephant pass by unheeded.
Again, is a man the slave of public opinion? Then
he will see no greatness in anything until it is recognised. Or, one of that numerous class who, like
'Bobus of Houndsditch,' worship, not talent, but 'the
power, cash, celebrity, or other success of talent'?
Then talent itself he would not know if he saw it.

But when we say that the Moral and Intellectual are one, the term 'Moral' is apt, perhaps, to
be misleading. It is associated in the common
mind with the mere external observance of the
Ten Commandments, and although this is indispensable to the well-being, nay, to the very
existence of society, we are liable to forget that it
is after all only the lowest form of morals, and may
coexist with the entire absence of all that constitutes nobility of soul. There is, no doubt, a feeling of hollowness attaching to any person of high
and refined qualities, who is wanting in a proper
sense of social obligations. He affects us as a
fine piece of architecture on rotten foundations.

And, indeed, we cannot too highly respect those solid virtues which lie at the root of all society. As a general rule, the man who respects the higher moral code will respect the lower. But exceptions must not be made too much of, or pressed too far. I do not defend Bacon or Goethe in their delinquencies, but I know, against all biography, that precisely what intellect they had, must have rested on and been proportioned to their moral qualities. The Ten Commandments, as I have said, are by no means a final code of morals. Christ found it necessary to ascend to a higher platform—the love of our neighbour. But it is still necessary to give even this a wider expansion, owing to the way it has been narrowed in its application. We have to ask of a man, not only, do you not steal, but also have you a sense of the high and noble wherever it is found ; have you a ₍wide and deep sympathy with all forms of life ; do you love truth for its own sake ; have you candour and tolerance, simplicity, humility, and magnanimity ? We have attained to magnanimity in warfare, and in every street row examples of it are to be seen. But the magnanimity that can make us disdain to show our wit or our knowledge at the expense of those weaker than ourselves, or to envy those more successful, is a rare virtue ; and is not found in those who merely keep the Ten Commandments, but in those who are possessed of the sublimer morals which we have seen to be the basis of all intellect. In the long run, the dependable man is the man of deep and sure insight, who sees the littleness of life, and of man, or of any man. But if your friend is the slave of public opinion, and his set of beliefs are such merely as society commends—his admirations, loves, and aversions regulated by it alone—then beware of him when the tide turns against you.

So clearly does Carlyle perceive that our insight is rooted in our moral virtues, that he regards these as the basis of all *literary* greatness. Force and fineness of understanding, he expressly asserts, are not distinct from general force and fineness of nature, or partly independent of them, but they always go together, except in special cases which are the result of special causes. His secret for being 'graphic' is simply to have 'an open loving heart and what follows from that.' There is no other secret for it that is worth having. He adheres to the old truth that love is the beginning of knowledge. The merit of originality is not novelty, but sincerity ' The believing man is the original man ; whatsoever he believes, he believes for himself, not for another.' In his life of Frederick the Great, he says, ' Better symptom of its quality human intellect cannot show for itself than that of gravitating to reality, to fact—not fiction.' He considers that 'the highest and only literary success is the virtue to produce belief.' ' For of all

feelings, states, principles of mind' he asks, with
great penetration, 'is not *belief* the clearest,
strongest, against which all others contend in
vain'? The power of imagination, the power of
invention, to be any evidence of intellect 'must be
invention of new truth, and has nothing to do with
fiction.' All mythologies were once philosophies,
were *believed.* Homer's Iliad, the Bible, were
believed ; and one of the highest merits of Shakspeare was 'the talent he showed of being able to
turn the History of England into a kind of Iliad,
almost perhaps into a kind of Bible.' All other
invention or imagination he thinks can be bought
cheap. Byron believed it could be had at any
time from an 'Irishman with whiskey in his head.'
He agrees with him who said that genius was
eternal patience. 'To swallow our disgusts, to do
faithfully the ugly commanded work, taking no
council with flesh and blood—Genius everywhere
in Nature means this, first of all, and without this
it means nothing—generally even less.' He could
have foreseen, he says, from Luther's greatness of
heart that he was a great thinker. 'Poetry' he
affirms 'is no separate faculty, no organ which can
be superadded to the rest, but rather the result of
their general harmony and completion.' A poet
without love he regards as an impossibility. He
advises the Literary Man to consider it well and
he will perhaps discover that ' The genuine "Art" in

all times is a higher synonym for God Almighty's
Facts—which come to us direct from Heaven, but
in so abstruse a condition, and cannot be read at
all, till the better intellect interpret them.' 'All
real Art is definable as Fact, or say as the disim
prisoned "Soul of Fact," and any other kind of
Art, Poetry, or High Art, is quite idle in comparison.' As all heroism rests on the same primary
qualities of mind and heart, all forms of it are convertible—the poet, prophet, priest, man of letters
and king.   Each has the raw material out of which
all the others are made, the difference in the form
being mainly due to circumstances.

As he regards the moral virtues as the basis
of intellect, so he regards intellect as the sum of
human worth. 'The end of intellect is to make
us *see* something, for this the whole man must co-
operate.' When he defines Shakspeare's faculty
as superiority of intellect, he says he has included
all under that. We have seen above that when
we attain to a clear insight into the World and our
duties in it, the feeling of Self-Renunciation dawns
on the mind. Otherwise, the passions, which must
be leashed in by some great controlling thought, are
liable to run riot. Speaking of Hoffman, Carlyle
says 'he found no sure principle of Action, no
Truth adequate to the guidance of such a mind.
He loved Art, not as the fountain of Beauty, but of
refined enjoyment ; demanded from it not peace,

but earthly excitement.' His weakness was in intellectual perception, which reacts on the character as the character reacts on it. 'He had not learned the Truth that for human souls a continuance of passive pleasure is inconceivable, has not only been denied us by Nature, but cannot, could not be granted.' We value men in proportion as their lives or writings show that they have gained the mastery over the lower elements of their nature. The egoism, gloom, and passion of Byron deduct from his greatness, and prove that he, too, had grasped no truth comprehensive enough to hold his passions in check. That is to say, he had not intellect *enough*. Add to him a few more profound convictions, a wider range of insight, and his whole procedure would have been different. His literary works would have been of another stamp, both in matter and treatment, and would have been as different from those we know, as the 'Meister's Travels' of the old Goethe is from the 'Sorrows of Werter' of his youth.

This doctrine of the unity of the Moral and Intellectual furnishes us with the key to Carlyle's biographies, and opens a new era in criticism. His conception of how a life should be written is a very lofty one. He demands that the biographer shall give us not separate features, but a portrait, not a catalogue of attributes, but their resultant as a living unity. And it must be admitted, that in his own practice he has realised this ideal. In this he differs greatly from his eminent contemporary, Macaulay, who floods his page with contradictory attributes, virtues and vices, the principal art displayed being their mechanical separation and arrangement into striking antitheses. This is only a superficial grouping of the outermost details of a character, and requires but ordinary insight. For, however significant the minutest circumstances may be, no addition of them in a Chinese catalogue will let us into their inner meaning. 'Wilt thou know a man' says Carlyle 'by stringing together beadrolls of what thou namest Facts? The man is the spirit he worked in, not what he did, but what he became.' To grasp this spirit requires a rare faculty. Besides the primary virtues of sincerity, candour, truthfulness, there must be that openness of mind, sympathy, or sensibility of nature that, by its own self-movement, realises the deep experiences of the heart. And as these are all moral attributes, they lend additional weight to Carlyle's doctrine of the dependence of the intellectual on the moral. But the drawing of character from the *outside*, by the mere accumulation or disposition of superficial details, requires no exceptional faculty. Differing from gossip only in its greater order and condensation, it is, like it, uninstructive, although 'perhaps entertaining and amusing. To say that an author's characters have such marked individualities that their prototypes are recognisable in a drawing-room, or in the street, is no high compliment. Shakspeare's great characters are not recognisable in the sense in which Pecksniff and Micawber are. We should not know Othello, but any jealous man is he in spirit. Shakspeare takes a central passion as his point of departure, and shows how it affects the whole nature, from the core to the most evanescent circumstance on the circumference. This is true also of Carlyle. By his wide intuitive sympathy, he feels about him until he gets into the motive spring of his hero's character, and works out from that. All the outermost facts are grouped and arranged around this central principle, and from it take their interpretation. Having found the nature of the moral principle,—its strength, compass, and elasticity—he proceeds to show that the intellectual power is commensurate. Thus, Voltaire has wide and keen sympathies, but is wanting in earnestness. and reverence. His intellect corresponds, being quick, clear, and many sided, but wanting in depth and solidity. Johnson's sincerity and courage, which are his central moral characteristics, appear in his intellect, which is characterised by strength of judgment and directness of insight. Schiller's intellect is refined and sublime, rather than broad or deep, corresponding to his moral nature which is pure and priestlike in character, but limited in sympathy. His want of sympathy with common things accounts for the almost entire absence of humour in his writings. Goethe, on the other hand, has the highest, deepest, and widest range of sympathies, and his intellect is as broad and manysided, as it is deep, aerial, and imaginative. Sir Walter Scott, again, is 'one of the healthiest of men,' a finely balanced organisation, with wide but common sympathies—not high, earnest or enthusiastic—and his intellect is in consequence picturesque, discursive, and graceful, but without elevation or intensity.

This doctrine of the identity of our moral and intellectual nature, is the vital bond that reunites those faculties of the mind which the metaphysicians had divorced. But the interpretation of the phenomena of life is incomplete, until we find the motive power by which this restless human activity is driven. We have still to ask, by what impulse the secret wheels of a man's nature are set in motion? Carlyle answers that we are driven by the Fantasy or the Imagination. This is his second great doctrine. It is freighted with the weightiest practical issues, and from it his views on Society and Government are derived. The life of man, from youth to age, is a fertile field for the illustration of this great truth. It is not the mere game or prize that the boy pursues with such avidity and delight, but it is the glittering charm, with which his imagination has surrounded it, that entrances his eye. The lover is not led by any mere beauty or grace, however transcendent, but by that divine ray, which he sees playing behind these, and which burns like a pillar of fire before his eager heart. The most sordid and calculating are no exception. The 'practical' man, the man of business, is as much the slave of his imagination as the most fervid and romantic enthusiast. He indignantly denies it, and protests that his mind can be moved only by the coldest prudence and caution. That he takes the safest path to his end within his power of vision, and in his choice of means is directed by judgment and discretion, may be admitted. But the end which sets in motion this agency of means, what is it but a fantasy? It is not the mere wealth, however colossal; it is not the mere success as it stands bare and uncovered, however overpowering; it is not the political measure as we know it when passed,—not the bald fact of negro emancipation or extension of the suffrage—but it is that mystic multi-coloured light, surrounding the fact and suffusing it, that enhances it in his imagination. It is fantasy, too, that leads those, who macerate themselves to obtain a position in society, an *entrée* into this or that distinguished circle, as well as those whose lives are spent in accomplishing great designs or forwarding the progress of science, art or letters.

In all these illustrations, we have, first, the object
to be attained, praiseworthy or not, and secondly
the idea which gathers round the object, but which
is distinct from it. That it is the *idea* and not
the bald *fact*, which we so eagerly pursue, is evident.
For if we take away the idea and leave the fact
unaltered, we can not be tempted to move. The
girl that we once loved and fondly fancied to have
gathered into herself the choicest excellences of
Nature, in whose presence we breathed a purer, a
diviner air, and who added a new and loftier
heaven to our life, we outgrow alas! the waxing
and exorbitant thought stealing away her charms,
as the cold unfeeling wind bereaves the tree of its
leaves and flowers. The political, literary or social
success which we hoped to attain, and which was
the light of our life through long years of struggle
and disappointment, comes at last, bringing with it
every thing, perhaps, that we expected, but the fancy
which endeared it to us. The book, too, which was
once our supreme delight, filling the eye and
running over the horizon on all sides, from which
we drank as from an exhaustless fountain, and
which seemed coextensive with Thought itself, we
gradually come up to, see its limitations, and at
last outgrow, leaving it behind, as the toys of our
childhood. Nothing that man can attain is final.
As soon as we come in possession of our idol, the
Divinity that hedged it in, flies away to objects more

·distant and unknown. This pursuit of illusions, as a chase of butterflies from flower to flower, is the good or evil genius of our life, and woos us to Heaven or Hell. 'Fantasy,' says Carlyle, 'I might call the true Heaven-gate or Hell-gate of man; his sensuous life is but the small temporary stage whereon thick-streaming influences from both these far yet near regions meet visibly and act tragedy and melodrama. Sense can support herself hand somely in most countries, for some eighteen pence a day; but for Fantasy, planets and solar systems will not suffice. Witness your Pyrrhus conquering the world yet drinking no better red wine than he had before.'

That it is the *idea*, and not the *fact*, which leads us on, becomes apparent when we recall the stages of life we have already outgrown. The boy smiles at the toys of his childhood; the youth at the frivolities that enchanted his boyhood; the adult at the sweet illusions that beguiled his youth. With every advance in culture, and at each stage of life, we require a new and less palpable temptation. The goddess Illusion is not to be jilted, and comes in all shapes and ·disguises, until she succeeds in captivating us. None escape her. Emerson says that, after reading books all his life, he is still the fool of every new page. This goddess by whom we are so willingly led, is the incentive to all exertion.

Without her inspiring influence, all enterprise and activity would droop and die. She is a most beautiful illustration of the skill with which the world is constructed.

This mystic halo which surrounds every object we pursue, is the light from that Divine Essence or Soul which works in, through, and behind all things. This is seen in the fact that it is always associated with the idea of excellence. Nothing low or grovelling, or that we fancy to be so, can lead us. 'Even for the basest sensualist,' asks Carlyle, 'What is sense but the implement of Fantasy; the vessel it drinks out of?' The object that can lay hold of our Fantasy must be a reflex, true or false, of those great attributes of the Soul—Beauty, Goodness, Justice, Truth,—of which Nature is the expression. The beauty of woman, suggesting an infinite grace and loveliness at the heart of Nature; the magnanimity of the hero, with his scorn of baseness and proud contempt of sensuous happiness; the unconquered heart of the martyr, silent in its sublime resignation; genius, consecrating with its sacred fire, the low, the wretched, the despised, or playing with the laws of life as with toys; these are all great in themselves, and well worthy of drawing on the imaginations of men. But there are others which more or less deceptively resemble these, and which are represented by social position or public recognition.

With the vulgar and the mass, these are the true
representatives of excellence and greatness. The
great attributes are believed to reside in kings, with
their power and majesty ; in the aristocracy, with
its grace, dignity, and easy condescension ; in men
of position and title, and in those whom the rever-
berations of fame have exalted in the general
imagination. But the important point is, that
these lay hold of the imagination because they are
believed to typify or embody that Divine Essence,—
pure, formless, impersonal,—which is more excellent
than any form. It is a curious illustration, too, of
the unity of the Mind, that whatever suggests that
high excellence which typifies the soul, suggests all
its forms. If we admire a man with our whole
heart, we unconsciously credit him with all excellence, and interpret or extenuate his vices in such
a way as to leave the impression of virtue. And
thus it is, that love, starting frequently from some
single quality—lofty expression, grace and beauty
of carriage or manners—suggests endless possibilities, endows its object with all excellence, and is
quite infinite in its nature.

That which within us is Imagination, in the
world outside of us is an Ideal. Ideals are thus
the soul and vital principle of our lives—our
activities and efforts in this world being their expression and embodiment. We admire, emulate,
imitate, follow, and endeavour to form our minds

F

to our ideals.   According to their character, therefore, is our life high or low, prosaic or poetic.   A
man's ideal may be read in the clothes he wears,
the house he builds, the company he keeps, the
society to which he belongs, the studies he prefers,
the actions he performs.   On the other hand, if we
know his ideal, we know all that is essential about
him.   We can predict, in a great measure, how he
will think, and how he will act, as we know, in a
general way, how a man will vote, when we know
the party to which he belongs.   'Show me the
man you honor,' says Carlyle, 'I know by that
symptom better than by any other what kind of a
man you yourself are.   For you show me there
what your ideal of manhood is ; what kind of a
man you long inexpressibly to be, and would thank
the gods with your whole soul for being if you
could.'   Ideals not only determine a man's worldly
aspirations and endeavours, but they reach to the
deepest recesses of his nature and determine also
his religion.   We have seen that Nature is the
expression of the Mind and Will of God, and that
every object in Nature (so intimate is the Unity
that pervades all things,) when deeply seen, reveals
the presence of God.   We have seen also that Man
is the epitome of Nature, and, gathering into himself all her excellences, is a clearer revelation of
God than any other work of creation.   The great
man, therefore, is the highest and clearest embodiment of the Godhead, and in so far as we admire,

love, and reverence him, do we worship God. For what worship can a man have in his soul for God, if he have none for God's likeness in his fellow-man ? The religions of the world grew out of the transcendent admiration of great men—Odin, Buddha, Mahomet. The divine attributes shone through these men with such transparent clearness, as to compel the admiration and worship of their fellows. 'Whatsoever Gods or Fetishes' says Carlyle 'a man may have about him and pay tithes to, and mumble prayers to, the real religion that is in him is his practical Hero-worship. Whom or what do you in your very soul admire and strive to imitate and emulate. Is it God's servant or the Devil's ? This is clearly the whole question.' Ideals constitute our religion, inasmuch as they are what we really believe in, rather than what we say we believe in. 'A man's religion consists not in the many things he is in doubt of, and tries to believe, but in the few he is assured of, and has no need of effort for believing.' As ideals thus determine our highest spiritual, as well as lowest temporal concerns, it is of the greatest moment that we should distinguish the true from the false. This is the great end of all education. In this, says Carlyle, all instruction begins and ends. True ideals are the embodiments of those attributes of God known as Justice, Beauty, Goodness, and Truth, and embrace art, literature, science, cultivated in a religious spirit,

and for high ends, and all noble self-sacrificing
work in any good cause.   False ideals, on the other
hand, are the embodiments of the lower side of our
nature, and comprise sordid love of money, selfish
ambition, love of applause, and love of power.
Those who aspire to the first, leave God's creation
fairer and better, and become themselves nearer in
likeness to the image of their Maker ; while those
who aspire to the latter, although their work is
converted into good, (for all things in Nature are
converted into good, even manure,) sacrifice the
soul to the body, and become themselves poor and
defaced.   'Honour Barabbas the Robber,' says
Carlyle, 'thou shalt sell old clothes through the
cities of the world, shalt accumulate sordid moneys
with a curse on every coin of them ; and be spit
upon for eighteen hundred years.'   To clear the
mind, so that we shall see what are high and noble
ideals, what are false and hollow, is thus the end of
all education.   All mere school and college learning, all scientific instruction, are poor and incomplete when divorced from this great end.   'Know
whom to honour and emulate and follow ; know
also whom to dishonour and avoid and coerce under
hatches as a foul rebellious thing, this is all the
Law and all the Prophets.   All conceivable
evangels, bibles, homiletics, liturgies and litanies
and temporal and spiritual law books for a man or
a people issue practically there.   Be right in this,

essentially you are not wrong in anything, you read the Universe tolerably aright and are in a way to interpret well what the will of its Maker is. Be wrong in this, had you liturgies the recommendablest in Nature, and bodies of Divinity as big as an Indiaman, it helps you not a whit, you are wrong in all things.' Around ideals the units of a Society aggregate, as iron-filings around a magnet. To estimate the worth of any Society, therefore, we ask what is its ideal? But as ideals differ in different ages and nations, a few remarks of a general character as to the conditions under which they arise may not be out of place here, and will serve as a connecting link between Carlyle's views of Man, and his views of Society and Government.

We may remark, first, that no ideal can be imposed on a man; he must either be educated up to it, or it must run in the line of his beliefs—either those he has been directly taught, those he has inhaled from the social atmosphere in which he lives, or those derived from his own observation, experience, or reflection. It is the same, too, with an age. The laurel crown of the Olympic games was an object of ambition alike to the highest as to the meanest citizen of Greece, and the victor's praises were commemorated in immortal verse by the first poets of the nation. The asceticism of the early Christian ages became the ideal of manhood, and the object of ambition of vast numbers,

and continued so for centuries. The chivalries and
tournaments, too, so felicitously described by Sir
Walter Scott, were once the models of excellence
to which all aspired. But these ideals of bygone
ages it would be impossible to graft on the present
world. By being kept in a strong glare before the
eye, they may raise all the feelings of admiration
and enthusiasm which are the stimulants to imita--
tion and exertion. But they are evanescent and
transitory. They are not supported by surrounding
opinion at the present hour, and no one takes the
first step, in consequence, towards their realisation.

We find, too, that as nations advance in civilisation and intelligence, their ideals ascend in
character. Among rude and early tribes the phy
sically strongest was most admired. When these
tribes were being welded into incipient nations, the
military hero naturally became the ideal. As
civilisation advanced, other attributes began to be
respected. In the time of Homer, strength and
subtlety, oratory and judgment, all received their
due share of homage, in Achilles, Ajax, Ulysses,
and Nestor. In the present day, physical strength is
quite secondary, the emphasis of admiration falling
on intellectual supremacy. Intelligence, by freeing
the mind from the trammels of superstition, gives
greater scope to individuality, and breaks the
uniformity of thought into a wide diversity of
forms. The sources of our admiration are, in con--

sequence, indefinitely multiplied ; and at the present time, we may reckon the ideals of eloquence, art, poetry, philosophy, politics, arms, and commerce.

This advance of ideals, which accompanies advancing intelligence, is retarded, however, by several potent causes. I shall here mention only two—National Utility, and the power of Organisation. These causes operate through Public Opinion, which in the long run determines the ideals that a nation will accept. We have to deal, therefore, not with the opinions of the most advanced and cultivated minds, but with that inert mass of passion, prejudice, interest and tradition, which makes up the intellectual outfit of what is called society. Now, Society keeps always on hand a stock of ready-made ideals, which the majority of young men accept without question, as if they were part of the ordinances of Nature. These stock-ideals are determined by National Utility and organised Power. The military ideal, for example, still holds its place in European society, from State-necessity, long after it has been outgrown by the progress of thought. The sword, which was once so essential to civilisation, now retards it, and yet the military man remains a choice ideal in society, and is admired, emulated, and courted, as much as any other. It is his importance as a State-machine that keeps this prejudice in his favour alive and active, and furnishes a ready-made ideal to the young ambitious mind. It is owing to the same cause that members of Parliament, returned in the majority of instances by length of purse, take what is called a 'position' in society out of all proportion to their personal merits. For it is of the first necessity that the Supreme Power in the State should be invested with due weight and dignity. The power that is acquired in the house by a clever speaker, and the career it opens, supplies another ideal to youth. Hence the prevalence of that ambitious figure—' the stump orator.'

The second great influence that determines the ideals of Society, is organised Power. All powerful organisations reflect a portion of their own dignity on the individual members. The leading offices in the Church-Hierarchy invest their holders with an importance and dignity in the public mind, which is denied to the solitary spiritual thinker, however transcendent; while, on the other hand, the members of the Press (which Carlyle regards as the real effective Church of the present day, but which is still *unorganised*) receive but scant admiration from society. The working classes, too, as a body, are flattered, precisely in proportion to their political power and the extent to which it is organised. Money itself is an organisation, and the great influence it exerts furnishes an ideal within the possible reach of the many. It, in consequence, attracts more devotees to its shrine than any other.

We have now arrived at the last division of our subject, viz. Carlyle's views on Society and Government. I do not intend to enter into a full consideration of this wide subject, which would require volumes, rather than a small portion of an essay. I shall merely confine myself to his leading lines of thought, and shall endeavour to arrange them in such a way, that they shall be seen to harmonise with, and follow from, all that has preceded. We have seen that every thought, feeling, or aspiration of the individual mind, has its visible exponent in action, word, or gesture. This outer visible ex pression of the inner invisible is figured by Carlyle as a *clothing*. Under the same figure, we may say that the thoughts, feelings, and aspirations of bodies of men, clothe themselves in visible organisations, by which they are rendered alive and active. Our widest spiritual concerns, for example, embody themselves in a Church, with its small outlying dependencies of missionary, tract, and bible societies. Our widest material interests embody themselves in Government, in which are included and protected all the lesser organisations of trade, commerce, and industry, with their shops, markets, and exchanges. Our intellectual activities which, in this age of division of labour, are so specialised, have built for themselves appropriate institutions— philosophical, scientific and literary. Our aesthetic faculties proper have provided, for their growth and expansion, theatres, operas, academies of music, and galleries of painting and sculpture. Our social feelings, too, have made for themselves clubs, coteries, and the institution of the family ; while, for the grosser excitements of our nature, we have betting, hunting, racing, and gambling associations.

These organised groups, in which Society embodies its feelings and aspirations, may be represented as lying, not along a *horizontal*, but a *vertical* line. This is the line of its ideals. Around the top are clustered the ranks, dignities, honors, and titles, which Society provides for its emulation and imitation, its admiration and worship. Around the bottom lie the gallows, prisons, and other more subtle, but equally deterrent punishments, provided for its censure or reprobation. If we carry the line upwards and downwards still farther, we shall come to Heaven and Hell ; for, as Carlyle profoundly remarks, 'not because Heaven existed did men know Good from Evil, the "because" I invite you to consider lay quite the other way. It was because men having hearts as well as stomachs, felt there and knew through all their being the difference between Good and Evil, that Heaven and Hell first came to exist.' But just as a man's ideal is the most important point about him, so the ideal of Society is its most significant feature. From this

we know whither all its aims, endeavours, aspirations, and efforts tend, and can at once determine
whether it is good or bad, healthy or diseased.
But before proceeding to examine the present
state of Society, I shall glance for a moment at
the significance of Society in itself, and the influ
ence it exerts over the individual mind. Growing,
as it does, mystically and mysteriously out of the
thoughts of men, it may be considered as a second
higher life surrounding our individual lives, and in
which all our powers find their arena and significance. It thus stamps its characteristic features
on its individual members, as an animal stamps its
features on its offspring. It imposes on us its prejudices, opinions, habitudes, and aspirations ; and
our education is, after all, only a superficial varnish,
which does not alter the original form, but disappears at a sufficient perspective. Here and there
we may meet with a man of haughty commanding
isolation, who disdains the yoke of contemporary
opinion, and who walks with a free unimpeded
step ; but the masses have no self-reliance. They
are kept erect, like the stones in an arch, by lateral
pressure merely, and would collapse if it were
withdrawn. The power of sympathy and the
sense of security which numbers afford is immense.
Carlyle often quotes the remark of Novalis that
' our *belief* gains quite infinitely in strength and
importance, the moment we can get others to agree

with us.' The solitary thought of the individual
mind is cold and transitory. The common thought
of multitudes, scattered far apart, is equally so.
Like separate faggots, though dry and combus-
tible, they are easily extinguished. But when
brought in contact, the smallest spark sets the
subtle flame a-leaping, and presently the whole is
enveloped in a wide-consuming blaze. Society is
thus omnipotent for good and evil, and its condi
tion is of immensely greater concern than that of
any individual. While, on the one hand, it
strengthens and intensifies noble thought and
noble action, on the other, it perpetuates idolatries,
error, and injustice. The thoughts of men who
were the lights of their age have fallen cold and
neglected on their contemporaries, while the arts
of some dexterous impostor, who understood scenic
effects and the disposition of costume, have stolen
men's admiration and worship. The anguish
which attends the withdrawal of public sympathy,
even for trivial causes, is another instance of the
powerful influence exerted by Society over the
individual. Society, too, tends to obliterate individuality by throwing its emphasis on conventional
abstractions rather than on personal distinctions.
It packs men into artificial categories, called
' classes,' for its own convenience, and attaches
labels to these, which serve to indicate the character of the contents. It does not countenance the

doctrine that Man is an immortal spirit with infinite possibilities, not to be gauged or exhausted, but regards him rather as a piece of *Jate*, attaching interest and importance to him, not as a man, but as a nobleman, clergyman, tradesman, working-man or footman. The truth is, this immense force, called Public Opinion, is not in itself a moral or divine force, although it stirs up the moral nature more than any other. It does not confer any divine 'sanction,' although it has practically the same effect, as we naturally believe that whatever everybody else believes or does must be right. But it is powerless against high virtue, and, when confronted by genuine greatness, proves blustering and impotent. And thus, Society, by generating Ideals, by fixing our moral conceptions whether true or false, by strengthening our beliefs, whether right or wrong, by stimulating action, whether good or bad, is of supreme importance. Carlyle recognises this, and his long line of historical works is intended to influence Society, perhaps, more than the individual.

With these somewhat trite remarks on the influence and general significance of Society, we have now to ask, what is the condition of Society at the present time, or in other words, what are its ideals? That which any nation believes with its whole heart, and with its whole heart strives to realise, is its ideal. It is the belief that has been powerful enough to reach the heart, and which is accepted as an axiom needing no demonstration or enforcing. An established reputation needs no heralding, an established business no advertisement. The Spartan needed no exhortation to courage; the Highlander, to devotion to his chief or clan; the Spaniard, or Scotchman, to veneration for his priest. 'What need of preaching patriotism' asks Carlyle, 'when the Decii were rushing with devoted bodies on the enemies of Rome?' But when Religion begins to decay, when Loyalty is dying out, and Patriotism is declining, then, proclamation of their beauty and virtue begins, and is heard far and wide. As we can read the prevailing crimes of an age from the old statute-books, so from the current preaching we can read the prevailing unbeliefs. If we ask what are the beliefs in the present age that need no enforcing, we can at once answer—belief in money, in applause, in position, in power. These are everywhere laid to heart and accepted as the ends and aims of life. On the other hand, while high virtues are so widely preached, to admit that you are working for a high and noble, but unremunerative ideal, to admit that your aim is not merely 'to get on in the world' but to attain to inward harmony, to religion and culture, is it not regarded by your friends as suicide and ruin? Sauerteig was not far off the mark, when he said, that 'the terror of not succeeding, of not making money, fame, or some other

figure in the world—chiefly of not making money,'
was the ' Hell of the English.'

We found that Society grouped its institutions
along a *vertical* line, which was the line of its ideals.
Properly speaking, this line splits itself into two.
One runs up to titles, rank, position, power and fame.
Along this steep and difficult ascent the feet of
the ambitious are seen laboriously plodding. The
dilettante in art, science, and literature, although
under quite other colours, is found on the same
road. The other line runs up to money, which,
being within the possible reach of the great multitude, is accordingly the most frequented highway
on earth. 'Mammonism' says Carlyle 'divides the
world with Dilettanteism.' A few devoted to high
and noble aims may also be seen going their own
way, but (although in these the hope and ideals of
the future lie) they may practically be left out of
account at the present time.

Carlyle, perceiving that Society is led by these
low ideals, pronounces it to be in a diseased, unhealthy condition, and predicts that it cannot continue. He assigns as the central cause of this unhealthy condition, the want of Religion. He says,
' you touch the focal centre of all our diseases, of
our frightful nosology of diseases, when you lay
your hand on this—There is no Religion, there is
no God.' Indeed, to say that Society is devoted to
selfish aims, is, in other words, to say that it is

devoid of Religion.   For there cannot be two an
tagonistic ideals in the soul at once, as each by its
nature absorbs the whole mind, and necessarily ex
cludes the other.   It is too literally true that we
cannot serve both God and Mammon.   A religious
Society is one that aims at high and noble ends
outside the range of individual self-interest; and
its health consists in working towards the aecom
plishing of these ends.   In former times, the religion of Society took the form of patriotism, of
loyalty to a person or institution, or of devotion to
a creed.   In the future, it will prescribe other
duties, suited to changed circumstances and condition.   But at the present time, Society is without
a religion, and the motto of all is 'each for him
self.'   This is evident to anyone who conscientiously
looks at what is passing around him.   The old
Church has unmistakably lost its hold on the best
minds, many of whom have withdrawn from it
altogether.   Of those who are still outwardly attached to it, the majority pay it but a lip-homage,
a conventional conformity.   Great numbers have
gone quite over to Materialism, and the secret un-
avowed scepticism of the last generation has come
to the surface, and is openly, sometimes boastfully,
paraded.   It therefore becomes the question of
questions for all earnest minds to consider, whether
Society can continue to exist without a belief in
God and Human Duty, or whether from the very

nature of things it must not inevitably fall to pieces. By Carlyle, this question is not regarded as of a merely hypothetical, speculative character, but as one that can be determined with scientific precision. Let us glance for a few moments at some of the leading lines of thought involved in it, and see in what direction they tend.

A body's individuality is maintained by the attraction of cohesion, which keeps its particles together and enables it to resist the disintegrating forces in and around it. If this cohesion is weakened or relaxed, the body loses its stability. Now, Religion does for Society, what the cohesive force does for matter. Society, in its strict sense, is the mutual union and co-operation of man with man, and is therefore *moral* by its very nature. Selfishness in all its forms, from the grossest to the most refined, divides men. Only love, justice, goodness, and truth can unite them. We love a man not for his selfishness, but for the unselfishness which we see or fancy we see in him. We cannot co-operate for any end, unless we subordinate our selfishness to the attainment of that end. The union will be real, and the self-sacrifice great, in proportion as our aim is high, our enthusiasm intense, and our sense of duty strong. But when Society has no aim outside of itself, but each individual works only for his own aggrandisement, every man's hand must be against his neighbour's, and Society cannot long continue. If we look at those associations of men of which Society is composed, we shall see how essential Duty and Virtue are to their very existence. What would become of a country if its soldiers were devoid of honour, and could be bought and sold like a horde of mercenaries, or were willing to sacrifice their country to their own personal safety? What would become of commerce and industry, if men could not be relied on to fulfil their engagements? The least want of confidence instantly affects markets and exchanges, and paralyzes the hand of Labour. The system of credit, which stimulates enterprise and multiplies wealth, is secure, only where the standard of commercial morality is high. The end of all literary, philosophical, or scientific societies would be frustrated, unless men were earnest in searching for truth, and truthful in reporting it. Not even a gambling or betting club could continue to exist, if its members were devoid of honour. If Charity were to stay her hand, hundreds would die daily of starvation or disease, and Society would be seriously endangered. Now, it is important to note, that these virtues, which are so essential to the very existence of Society, (especially in our highly complex state of civilization) are prescribed by Religion, and are held sacred, in proportion as Religion is believed. The root of all religion is the belief in God. The essence of all duty and virtue is obedience to His

Laws, founded on that belief. The decay of Religion is the death-blow to Duty and Virtue, as the
excision of the roots is the death of the tree. But
it may be contended that there is in Man a principle of reverence, goodness, truth, and justice,
which is as natural and spontaneous as the love of
pleasure or self interest, and which can no more be
rooted out by atheism, than the passions can be
by asceticism ; that these virtues will always arise
when they are wanted, and by furnishing that
cohesive force which is necessary to keep our selfishness in check, will preserve the equilibrium of
Society. Now, it is most important that the truth
which this view contains, should be separated from
the error. There can be no doubt that Nature, in
the widest sense of that term, has no intention of
breaking up or retrograding, and that she will
therefore throw out such balances as are necessary
for her own great ends. But it is quite a different
matter with an individual or a nation. The human
body, for example, is so constructed that in walking there is a perfect self poise at every point ; but
if from carelessness, indifference, or conscious
intention, we overbalance ourselves, the slightest
push will bring us to the ground. It is the same,
too, with our moral nature. The mind of every
sane healthy man is provided with a moral nature
as the balance to his selfishness, but as we so often
see, it may become seared, deadened and even

obliterated ; no balance being thrown out to stay
the inevitable consequences of laws that have
been violated. The thief, the murderer, and the
drunkard slide gradually down the slippery de-
scent, each delinquency smoothing the way for a
greater, until ruin embraces them. The like holds
true with nations. Take, for example, the fall of
Rome. With religion dead, and augurs winking at
each other; with Society destitute of patriotism,
loyalty, public and private principle ; with wealth
and poverty confronting one another in huge un-
sympathetic masses ; what could happen but that
she should stagger and stumble from bad to worse,
until she was swept out of existence ? The condition of France before the Revolution, affords
another pregnant and instructive example of the
same thing. For Religion is the director of Man's
mind, as the mind is the director of his body. A man
might as well attempt to guide himself with his feet
and walk with his head, as a nation to guide
itself with selfishness elevated into a religion.

The doctrine of the Materialists, too, demands
a passing consideration. It is contended by them
that a man's self-interest acting on an enlightened
judgment, will, as a mere matter of prudential calculation, cause him to respect the rights of others,
while insisting on his own. This is not even true
of individuals, much less of the classes into which
Society is divided. For, as a matter of fact, in a

Society devoid of Religion, it is only where the powers of contending interests are nearly equal, that there is the least chance of their being re-spected, like the compromise of bullies who are uncertain of each other's strength. But where *power* is unequal, legislation from its very nature must follow power. For some centuries the Aris-tocracy were more powerful than the Commons, but no 'enlightened Self-interest' made them respect the rights of others, while insisting on their own. Each and every right had to be extorted from them, sometimes even at the point of the sword. And when power shall have passed over to the People, in reality as well as in name, the Aristocracy will have to whistle for their rights, if they have nothing more to rely on than the 'enlightened self-interest' of those to whose in-terests they are opposed. Indeed, so little faith have we, at present, in the 'enlightened self-interest' of others, that we are made aware by a fatal instinct, that over and above the rights which the law allows us, we have no chance of any other rights in this world, except by looking well after our own interests; which we accordingly do.

But the Materialists also contend that the duty and virtue at present existing in Society are, at bottom, only a *form* of that same 'enlightened self-interest.' Carlyle denies this, (and it behoves all earnest minds to consider well these two oppo-

site views,) and affirms, on the contrary, that they
are the result of the religious teaching of the past ;.
that the commercial morality which is still very
high among us, compared with many other nations ;.
that loyalty, patriotism, and honour, (equally with
the laws that thou shalt not kill or commit adul-
tery,) have been slowly built up by religious pre-
cept, have been enforced by religion, sanctioned
by religion, and transmitted to us, like all our habitudes, customs, and modes of thought and procedure. The young mind inhales them with his life's
breath, and pays them respect, in proportion as he
finds them held sacred by that corporate individual,.
which is no one and yet every one, named Society.
These virtues will linger, like idle ceremonies that
have lost their meaning, long after the religion,
which prescribed them has become extinct, but in
the end, like them, must perish. At the present
time, everybody professes to believe in the necessity of duty, of straightforwardness, of honesty,.
and of doing good. The most advanced atheists.
have not as yet ventured to reject these fundamental virtues. But as they have no vital principle
when Religion is gone, what can keep them alive ?
Thoughtful men will ask themselves, what is the
use of performing disagreeable duties that have no.
religious sanction ; and, while keeping up a show
of belief, will secretly devise means of shirking the
onerous tasks which interfere with their comfort.

and pleasure. Each will try to feather his own nest, while still preaching duty to everybody else, lest they should insist on sharing his spoils. In the meantime, money, ambition, and power, which directly gratify selfishness and vanity, will be seen to be the only good, as indeed they must be if there is nothing higher. With a selfishness increasing in intensity as the sense of duty and virtue declines, the laws of honour, of commercial morality, the sacredness of the marriage bond and of personal integrity will become more and more weakened and relaxed. Then will begin to appear the legitimate and necessary consequences of disbelief in God and Religion. The consciousness of having a sympathetic audience will give boldness to those who have long felt, that Religion being dead and buried, Duty was an obsolete impertinence. Convictions that had long been secretly cherished will now be openly avowed, and duty, virtue, and morality, as in the French Revolution, will be ignominiously ejected.

This rapid decomposition which follows the loss of religious belief is accelerated by the onward tread of Democracy. When money, independence, luxury, and love of power become the ends of a people, Democracy tends to establish itself, and is a mighty additional element of disruption. It is a grand and everlasting ' right of Man ' that no factitious advantage should be given to any class, creed,

or organised body in the State, but that a paved
and open thoroughfare should lead, from every man's
threshold, to an arena where his intellectual and
moral nature shall have full power to expand to its
utmost limits, and where every facility shall be given
him of taking that place among his fellow-men to
which by merit he is entitled. The democracy
that aims at this great end, is high and glorious, and
every effort made to realise it is worthy of support.
But, observe, that where the motto is 'each for himself,' and 'Devil take the hindmost,' democracy
cannot stop here. Every extension of the suffrage
throws power into the hands of those less and less
capable of exercising it wisely, that is to say, for
any other purpose than their own interests; until
with Universal-Suffrage there is nothing to control
the passions of a self-interested, ignorant, and irre-
ligious mob. John Stuart Mill, the clearest-
sighted of the materialists, foresaw this inevitable
result, and advised such checks as the 'representation of minorities' and 'plurality of votes.' But
when the power is once obtained, it will not, on the
principle of self-interest, submit to such checks,
but will be abused, as that of the aristocracy was
before it. Mr. Gladstone advocates the extension
of the suffrage, mainly on the ground that it has
been historically beneficial, and that there is such
an innate reverence among the lower orders for
their 'superiors,' that any power put into their

hands would not practically be abused. But I fear this is a fond imagination. The fallacy lies in not sufficiently allowing for the element of *time*. He should have gone back as far as the Tudors, rather than only to the first Reform Bill. Since the time of Henry the Eighth, every popular right has been won by *power*, or in other words, by a real, if not nominal, extension of the suffrage. But at the present time, what has become of the power, or if you like, the ancient rights of the Aristocracy and Crown? Have the rights *gained* by the People not been *taken away* from the Nobility? It is beyond the region of doubt, that as religion declines and self-interest increases, loyalty to superiors cannot long continue, and that a universal-suffrage without a religion must hasten the decomposition of Society.

Hence Carlyle's denunciations of Democracy, and of Parliamentary Government as the temporary halting-place on the road to it. In considering Carlyle's ideas on Government, it is important to bear in mind that his eyes are fastened on the future, rather than on the present. The point with him is not with how little parliamentary jolting we are getting along, but the goal to which we are hastening. As we drift so pleasantly along the sunny stream, he warns us of the Niagara that lies before us. A glance at some of the broad characteristics of Parliamentary Government may serve to bring into greater prominence the wide divergence of opinion that separates him from his own age. The first thing we have to remark of Parliamen tary Government is, that, as it exists to represent the different *interests* of Society, legislation must follow the line of greatest *power*, as in physics, a body acted on by opposing forces follows the line of their *resultant*. Previous to the passing of the first Reform Bill, for example, the landed Aristocracy controlled the Legislature, and legislation accordingly, after a superficial play of logic-fence, eventuated in measures for the interest of that powerful body ; with a sop thrown in occasionally to appease the drowsy masses when they began to growl. The Reform Bill itself was the outcome of the conflict of interests that had reached a climax, and was the symptom that power had passed over to the Middle Classes. The first practical result of this conversion of potential into actual power was the decay of the House of Lords, which was stripped of its ancient political authority. This slice cut off the *political* interests of the Aristocracy was followed by a slice off their *commercial* interests, in the repeal of the Corn Laws. The Church too would, in all probability, have shared the same fate, had it not been bound up with the feelings of a large section of the Middle Classes, as well as with the whole Aristocratic régime. Its disestablish- ment now only awaits the return of a sufficient number of members pledged to the interests of Nonconformity. This play of opposing *interests* is made respectable by dignifying it as a conflict of *rights.* But that Parliament exists to represent interests, and not rights, is seen in the way members are returned. They are returned primarily in the interests of a particular party—the Conservatives, to hold on to what they already possess, the Liberals, to take from them their prerogatives, and apply them to their own interests. Besides this primary object, members are returned in the special interests of locality or trade—as the Irish interests, the manufacturing or agricultural interests, the interests of consumer or producer. These minor interests try to secure the co-operation of one or other of the major interests of Conservatism or Reform, and legislation as before is the mathematical *resultant* of the powers engaged.

The next point to be noted about Parliamentary Government is that it drifts *aimlessly* without a rudder down the stream of time. As the legislature is the reflex of the people, so the government is the reflex of the legislature. With a cabinet merely to carry out the wishes of the legislature, and a legislature to carry out the wishes of the people, the age of statesmanship is gone. It is replaced by the meaner arts of adroitness and diplomacy. A Conservative Premier, as the representative of power that, on the whole, is

losing ground, requires perhaps an excess of adroit
ness; a Liberal Premier, as the representative of
power that is gaining ground, an excess of bold
ness.   But neither require commanding insight.
The complaint which we sometimes hear, that so
few intellectual men are returned to Parliament, is
purely gratuitous.   The world may be trusted to
know what it wants.   They are not returned because they are not needed there.   To steer the
Ship-of-State requires a high order of intellect
and a far-reaching power of vision; the ability it
requires differs as much from what Carlyle calls
steering by the *ear* (by the voices from the surrounding benches, and the shouts of the people
from the shore through the *Times*) as the insight of
the cultivated physician, who treats symptoms with
a wide view of their relation to the whole, differs
from the empiric, who, when his patient cries out,
puts a soothing-plaster over the seat of pain.   To
Carlyle, the whole forms a melancholy spectacle as
it drifts along the rapids towards the Niagara of
Democracy.   In front the figure-head of the
Crown; behind it, the Cabinet pushed on by the
Legislature; and drawing up the rear, the jostling
noisy multitude pushing all before it.

That the present form of Parliamentary Government is drifting towards Democracy is unquestionable.   Every extension of the suffrage brings
it a stage nearer.   Formerly the Aristocracy con-

trolled legislation, then the Middle Classes. But
the late extension of the suffrage to a part of the
Working Class, and the flattery that attends it,
indicate too well where the balance of political
power will lie in the future. The pointers on the
dial plate of legislation, which are thus of themselves veering towards democracy, are accelerated
by the wide-spread belief that democracy is the
'Cause of Man,' and for the well-being of all. The
consequence is that an extension of the suffrage,
which formerly followed the appearance on the
horizon of a new and menacing political power,
now has a tendency to anticipate it. The extreme
enthusiast would thrust Universal-Suffrage on us
without any regard whatever to the condition of
the masses ; the more moderate, only after they
were sufficiently educated to receive it. But both
believe that the possession of the suffrage is in
itself a training for its wise exercise. If it is
meant that they will use it intelligently for their
own interests, the point is at once conceded. But
if it means that they will respect the rights of
those whose interests are opposed to their own, it
is questionable, even deniable. The aristocracy
have always had sufficient intelligence to exercise
their power wisely, but the fact is, they have always
used it for their own interests. So too have the
middle-classes. What reason then, is there, for
supposing that the lower-classes will act otherwise?

There is still, doubtless, among the lower-classes a large measure of virtue. There is still a strong sense of duty, and a religion that, at all events, takes the form of a genuine respect and reverence for their 'superiors.' Now, these are all conservative forces, and give Society cohesion. They also maintain the balance of power in the upper and middle classes. But when Universal-Suffrage throws the balance of political power into the hands of the masses, and demagogues begin to play upon them, (and power that is flattered soon forgets that it has superiors,) to believe that they will not force legislation along the line of their own interests, is contrary to all experience of Parliamentary Government.

If we turn to Carlyle's ideal of Society and Government, a striking contrast presents itself. Instead of Society being a conflict of opposing interests, it is to be a state of mutual helpfulness ; instead of Religion being merely the policeman's assistant, it is to be the inspirer of our lives ; instead of the Ship-of-State being allowed to drift about, blown hither and thither by popular passion, it is to be steered by Great Men, guided by the pole star of Eternal Truth. We have now to ask how this New Era is to be inaugurated, what are the conditions necessary to its existence, and how it is practically to be realised ? But before entering into Carlyle's views on this subject, it is necessary to point out that it is only in the far distant future that he looks for its realisation. It is the Ideal to which Society, by straight or crooked paths, must ultimately attain ; the realising of that Kingdom of God on earth, for which the good and great of all ·ages have sighed, but sighed in vain. It is the Golden Age of the world, which lies in the future, not in the past. Carlyle's views have been renounced by many, as being impracticable in the present stage of Society. But his critics have forgotten that he has distinctly stated that there is not the slightest chance of their being realised, except by a total change in our present aims and aspirations. He confesses that he has no ' Morrison's Pill ' for the present ills of Society. We must have a total change of regimen. Our way of life must be completely altered. If Society is for ever to be given over to the conflict of self interests, ' cloaked under due forms of war, named " Fair Competition," " Supply and Demand,"' he candidly admits that there is no hope of the New Era. But as he regards the present stage of Society as transitional, and foresees that it must either reform itself or be annihilated, he lifts up his Ideal from afar, as the haven to which we must steer for safety.

In every Society that is not destroyed by foreign conquest or reduced to slavery, while the old Forms are being cast off, the germ of a new

order of things is slowly forming beneath. This
germ is Religion, which is the keystone of Society.
The first essential therefore of the New Era is
that we regain the Religion, which we have lost.
This is itself a work of ages. With Materialism
not so much militant as triumphant; with Duty
and Virtue reduced to the *caput-mortuum* of self-
interest; and the Old Church split up into a number of jangling sects; a long time must elapse
before the intellects of men can be brought into
harmony with their spiritual intuitions. In the
section in which I have treated of Carlyle's Religion, are embodied the essentials of *the Religion
of the Future.* As we have seen it is not a new
Religion, but is the essence of the old, freed
from the superficial adhesions and encrustations
which have become incredible to the modern mind.
It consists in the knowledge and clear insight
that at the bottom of all the contradictions of
Time, there is a God who is all-Just, all-Beautiful;
that it is our duty to *renounce* ourselves and submit to His will; to love our neighbour; and to
convert all our principles into Conduct and Action.
When Science, hitherto the most powerful instrument in destroying the old *forms* of Religion, gets
an eye for the *whole*, instead of losing herself as
at present among the bewildering details, she will
become the most powerful support of Religion.
But Religion has a more powerful antagonist than

Science, and that is Public Opinion. This is and has always been her greatest rival. The truth is Public Opinion is Society's real religion. But the gods of this world are not the true gods. The religion of Society is not the true religion. It is no doubt difficult for the ordinary worldling to believe, that Society will ever have different aims from those it has at present. Nevertheless, those who have had deep religious experiences, know that it is quite conceivable, nay credible. And what one man knows, all in time may. In those seasons of religious excitement which ever and anon visit communities, the things of this world are burnt as a scroll, in the fierce heat of the Eternal. And even in that more equable glow of religious conviction, which warms the heart and refreshes like light, men rise above the low aims of their contemporaries. It is not impossible, then, to conceive that, in time, Society shall have regained her Religion. The first effect of a Society imbued with Religion, would be the dethronement of the ' Money-bag of Mammon.' Or, perhaps, it were more correct to say that the two processes would go on simultaneously, as the machinery of Society must always adapt itself to the changes in its vital conditions. The brute-god of Physical Force has been dethroned, why should not Mammon likewise be? In the early stages of Society, physical strength was the test of manhood. Ad-

H

miration and emulation, in consequence, followed
personal prowess. We may see a remnant of this
among the lowest class of our population, even in
our own day. As late as the Middle Ages, the
barbarians who overran Europe, settled matters of
Right and Wrong, and adjusted personal disputes,
by physical force. In the 'trial by combat,' it was
believed that God would defend the right. But
the right man was the 'best man,' as we say, or the
one who was successful in a personal encounter.
In the present day, the display of physical superiority confers no honour, and is not emulated or
esteemed. Physical force has been replaced by
a more subtle gauge of manhood. Our admiration and emulation now follow the man who can
make most money. The consequence is, that men
sweat and jostle, wearing away both soul and body
in the scramble for wealth. Is it impossible then
to conceive that in a Society imbued with Religion,
the possession of money should be as little a mark
for our admiration, as is now the possession of
physical strength? For the progress of Society
consists precisely in this—that the lower attributes
of our nature are, one by one, degraded in esti-
mation, and the emphasis falls on higher qualities.
From the lowest savage to the highest civilised
being, the poles of Man's nature are the same
— *good* and *evil, admiration* and *reprobation,
greatness* and *meanness, heaven* and *hell.* The ad-

vance of intelligence consists in more accurately classifying the aims, endeavours, thoughts, and actions, that are to occupy these poles ; as the progress of Science consists in more accurately classifying the endless variety of animals and plants under their proper species and genera. To find, by a deeper insight into life, *what* is good, and *what* is evil ; what ought to be admired, and what reprobated ; what should be the heaven, and what the hell of a man ; and to conform Society to it, is the end of all science, thought, and legislation among men. At one time, as we have said, *personal prowess* was the greatest good of a man, was his heaven and ideal. In the New Era it is to be *wisdom* and *virtue.* A man's hell was once *physical inferiority*, but in the New Era it will be *stupidity, moral obliquity*, and a *selfish, animal existence.* But in the present transitionary stage of Society, the heaven or ideal is mixed, as is also the hell or reprobation. The ideal is *intellect* and *virtue*, with the accessories of money, position, fame, power ; but you will note that, practically, the greatest weight is attached to the accessories. The hell or reprobation is *poverty*, with the accessories of crime, baseness, selfishness ; the emphasis (if we judge by action, not by sentiment) falling on the poverty.

But with a Religion that throws our ideal on Wisdom, Moral Worth, and Noble Action ; and our

reprobation on the opposites of these virtues, Society
will have an aim outside self-interest. It may be
objected, that, unless each individual can secure
what he works for, the hand of Labour will be
paralysed. But if we consider it, it is not so much
the reward of labour, in its material sense, that
men prize, as the honour, dignity, and power, which
it can procure. The objection, therefore, has no
weight, when applied to a state of society, in which,
by the hypothesis, there is no honour attaching to
the possession of wealth. It may also be objected,
that, although we have thrown out self-interest (in
the shape of money,) as an aim, Vanity, which is the
most subtle form of selfishness, will still elude us ;
and ambition, hypocrisy, and all their train will not
have been eradicated, but only have changed their
form. To this it may be replied, that, although it
is impossible to root out of the human heart the
love of esteem, under the influence of Religion it
assumes the nobler form of love of sympathy, and
loses its vulgar and selfish character. Besides, as
wisdom is the aim, there is no sphere for vanity.
It is only by subordinating our selfishness, that we
can ever attain to true wisdom. If there is any
truth in Carlyle's doctrine of the dependence of the
intellectual on the moral, vanity must either take
a nobler form, or disappear altogether. Nor will
there be any field for the Demagogue, or 'Stump-
orator,' in a society where the characteristic of

Religion is Work, and where Speech, unless converted into Action, is worthless and of no influence ; nor for the Political Economist, where the end is mutual helpfulness, and not self-interest, competition, supply-and-demand ; nor for the Materialist and Mechanical Philosopher, where Duty and Virtue are known and felt in the heart to be divine. But, of course, the truths of universal application, which they have discovered, will be embodied in the general stock of human knowledge, and on them Society will stand and work.

Society, then, having attained a Religion of Work, we now want to know what it is to work at. This requires two things. We must know what are the Tendencies of the World, or the Laws of God ; and also what are the special wants of the time. For this we require the man of deep insight, and wide prophetic vision. He it is who can best interpret the Will of God to men ; and best bring the affairs of men into harmony with the Will of God. To reverence and loyally follow him, is our duty and highest privilege. Hero-worship does not seem to be in high repute, in this age of independence of thought. There is such a variety of opinion on every subject, human and divine, that we have agreed to differ, and each to follow his own nose. Nevertheless, Hero-worship is in as full play as ever it was, only nothing comes of it. In renouncing Hero-worship, men do notthe less admire and worship. Each has his own idolatry, but is suspicious of that of his neighbour. Hence there is no united action to any great end. Besides, as Society has no aim outside the self-interest of its members, it does not require to be led by heroes. It asks from its governors, not so much guidance, as passive obedience to its will. But in a Society that wishes to steer to a certain point, to attain an object outside of itself, Hero-worship at once establishes itself, as in France under Buonaparte. A hierarchy of command and obedience necessarily ensues, and what may be called the aristocratic form of society tends to establish itself. Besides, where the aim of each is not personal and peculiar, but common to all, a unanimity of opinion would be more easily attained, and the best men would be readily found. If we take those associations that exist for the discovery of Truth, as scientific, literary and philosophical societies, we shall find that the best men are soon known. All the members, pursuing the same inquiries, and being animated by the same aims, the men whose knowledge is most extensive are at once recognised. They are accordingly appointed to the posts of honour, and are loyally revered. The same, too, would be the case in a nation that pursued high and unselfish aims. But when the object is self-interest, there is no hope of finding the best man, or of his being reverenced

when found. In America, the President's chair is
filled by the man·who has made himself least obnoxious to the general interests of his party, and
who can command the greatest number of votes.

Looking over Society at the present time, we
have to ask, what part of its business has to be put
into harmony with the Laws of God. The first
thing that strikes us is the question of Labour.
Its motto at present is 'Each for himself,' and its
law, 'Cash is the sole nexus between man and
man.' Men count their coins, as Indians their
scalps, and are admired and worshipped accordingly. The consequence is, that, although wealth
has increased beyond example, three-fourths of
mankind spend their lives in the inglorious struggle
against want. But the Law of God is, that only in
'mutual helpfulness' is Society possible. At present our mutual helpfulness goes to the extent of
throwing a penny into the hat for soup-kitchens,
poor-houses, and the conversion of the heathen.
Some fairer distribution of the products of Labour
is imperatively demanded by the Law of God.
Labour must not be left in its present 'Chactaw'
condition, but, in Carlyle's words, must be 'made a
chivalry of.' For the epic is not now 'Arms and
the Man,' but 'Tools and the Man.' In the New
Era, men will be admired, not for what they have
succeeded in clutching for themselves, but for the
noble manner in which they have distributed it

among their fellows. The next most pressing demands are Education and Emigration. 'Is it not
scandalous to consider' writes Carlyle in 1843
'that a Prime Minister could raise within the year,
as I have seen it done, a Hundred and Twenty
Millions Sterling to shoot the French; and we are
stopped short for want of the hundredth part of
that to keep the English living? The bodies of
the English living, and the souls of the English
living; these two " Services" an Education Service
and an Emigration Service, these with others will
actually have to be organised.' Carlyle does not
go into detail on any of these questions. He
admits that it is impossible to foresee more
than the general direction which legislation ought
to take, but considers that, if men were willing,
there would be little difficulty in devising machinery
to meet the ends.

EMERSON.

THERE is perhaps no. writer of the nineteenth century who will better repay a careful and prolonged perusal than Emerson. He enjoys the rare distinction of having ascended to the highest point to which the human mind can climb—to the point where, as he says of Plato, the poles of thought are on a line with the axis on which the frame of things revolves. From this elevation, he has given us his views of the World, of Man, and of Society. But, unfortunately, he has not chosen to lead us up to his own point of view by a connected chain of thought. Hence the difficulty we find in reading him. Thinkers like Comte and Mill have done us the honour of admitting us to the recesses of their minds, and of allowing us to see the processes by which they arrived at their views of the World. In doing so, they have furnished us with the key to their special opinions. Had Emerson given us, at the outset, a general outline of his philosophy, his pages would have been more intelligible. As it is, we are as much in the dark, on a first perusal, as we should be in

attempting to read the *Principia* before mastering
the steps that lead up to it. Having finished his
thinking before he commenced writing, he has
drawn up the ladder by which he ascended, and
sits uttering his oracles in solitary isolation. The
consequence is, that the brilliant exhibitions of
thought and metaphor, puzzle and surprise, rather
than edify us. These difficulties are aggravated
by the way in which he treats his subjects. The
topics are the ordinary concerns of life—experience, prudence, character, heroism, friendship,
wealth, beauty, and the like. We open the book
anticipating little difficulty from such trite and
well-worn themes. But we are quickly unde-
ceived. The first sentence will very likely stagger
us, and we are fortunate if the succeeding ones do
not increase our mystification. The thoughts are
not consecutive, and have as little connexion, it
has been said, as if they had been scattered out
of a pepper-box. He passes rapidly from point
to point, without any of those easy transitions and
connecting links that indicate the way we are
travelling, and apprise us of any change in the
point of view. He never dilates or amplifies, but
condenses a chapter into a paragraph. Each
sentence might form the text of an ordinary discourse. His illustrations, even, have often as little
apparent connexion with the thought, as the
thought has with the subject. Some of them

would exemplify equally well any number of different principles. Others, again, are themselves generalizations, and must not be construed literally. The whole body of thought is so overlaid with metaphor, that we have difficulty in recognizing its true character.

The key to this procedure is to be found in his intellectual standpoint. He does not arrange his facts according to their outward or *logical* relations, but according to their inner *spiritual* affinities. He stations himself at the point where the ascending lines of Law (on which the diversity of physical and moral phenomena are strung) pass into Unity. Once attain to that position, and every sentence becomes luminous The connexion of ideas becomes apparent; the illustrations are seen to be pertinent and exact; and the subject to be laid open on all sides by direct and penetrating insight. We can then return to him, with the same delight, for the philosophical expression of the deep laws of human life, as we do to Shakspeare for their dramatic representation. For he is one of the profoundest of thinkers, and has that universality, serenity, and cosmopolitan breadth of comprehension, that place him among the great of all ages. He has swallowed all his predecessors, and converted them into nutriment for himself. He is as subtle and delicate, too, as he is broad and massive, and possesses a practical

wisdom and keenness of observation, that hold his
feet fast to the solid earth, when his head is
striking the stars. His scientific accuracy and
freedom of speculation mark him out as one of
the representative men of the nineteenth century.
We cannot afford, therefore, to lose thoughts of
so much weight and importance, through imperfect
apprehension. We must not be daunted by the
difficulties attending a first or second perusal.
With patience, light begins to dawn on us ; and
with light, hope. With the reader's indulgence, I
shall endeavour in the following pages to gather
up a few of the larger fragments of connected
thought which he has let fall by the way, in the
hope of being able to lighten a little the difficulties
of interpretation and to follow the steps by which
he ascended to the Temple of Philosophy.

Emerson is associated in the popular mind
with Carlvle. By some, his works are regarded
as a weak and diluted, by others, as a strong
and concentrated form of the writings of that
distinguished thinker. This is, of course, a mere
superstition. They both belong, it is true, to
the same class of spiritual or intuitive thinkers.
Their general views of Man and Nature are alike.
Neither of them is a logician or metaphysician, in
the ordinary acceptation of the term. Both have
pierced through the contradictions of life, and have
centered themselves in the divine Unity. But they
owe little to each other, although, like other great

men, they are deeply indebted to their predecessors. Their disagreement is more marked than their agreement. Their speculative views are almost identical, but in their practical application of these views, there is the most striking antagonism. Carlyle is the exponent of Despotism, in the best sense of that term ; Emerson, of Liberty ; and to these opposite principles, which re-appear in every Society, they have respectively given the deepest philosophical basis. I have accordingly regarded a study of Emerson as a fitting sequel to a study of Carlyle. But as I wish to avail myself of every mode of statement that will help to strengthen those views of the World which it is the main object of this volume to enforce, I have deemed it expedient to develop Emerson's views of Nature and Man at some length. When I arrive at the point where he parts company with Carlyle, I shall consider their views together, and endeavour, by contrast, to bring into clearer relief the characteristic differences between them.

In his mode of representing Nature, Emerson belongs to the school of Idealism. The distinctive doctrine of this school of thought will be more clearly seen, perhaps, if we contrast it with the opposite doctrine of Materialism. The Materialist considers Man as a *product* or outcome of an order in Nature, that exists and would exist independently of himself. The Idealist, on the con-

trary, considers Man as the centre of Nature, and
his mind as the point from which all things (including the Laws of Nature) take their interpretation.   Since the advent of modern Scientific
Materialism, it must be admitted that Idealism
has been under a temporary eclipse.   Nevertheless,
it may be confidently asserted, that around the
widest ring of Materialism, a ring of Idealism may
be drawn.   'Every Materialist' says Emerson
'will be an Idealist, but an Idealist can never go
backward to be a Materialist.'   To make good
this statement, it is not necessary to examine in
detail the different systems of Materialism that
have appeared in the world.   They have all a
common basis, and it is in this basis that the weakness lies.   That it should have been so persistently
overlooked by materialists themselves is only to be
accounted for by the fact that they have neglected
to examine their foundations, in their zeal to rear
an imposing and symmetrical superstructure.   Let
us examine for a moment, the doctrine which lies
at the base of all Materialism, viz. that Mind, being
an attribute of nervous action, is, like it, explained
and accounted for by the physical laws of Nature.
In setting out to investigate the relation between
Mind and Matter, the conscientious Materialist,
after clearing from his mind all preconceived
hypotheses, determines to follow the true Baconian
method, and base his conclusions on the observa-

tion of facts, and of facts only. As the result of a long series of experiments and observations, he finds that from the first dawning of consciousness in the lower creation, up to its noon-splendour in Man, there is an exact correspondence between the mental manifestations and the condition of the nervous centres. Whatever else varies, this relation remains constant throughout his investigation. He feels justified, therefore, in drawing the conclusion, that Mind is merely one among other mani festations of the laws of Matter. Now, this con clusion, reached inductively, is afterwards made use of deductively, to solve some of the deepest human problems. It is carried about as a lamp to throw light on the great questions of Immortality, of the existence of God, of Final Cause, and of the nature of the First Cause. It is therefore all the more essential that the fallacy in it should be clearly pointed out. It lies, in short, in the materialist's assuming that only *one* element goes to make up his conclusion, whereas, there are really *two*. The element on which he entirely bases his conclusion is the series of facts observed. But there is a second element which he completely ignores, viz.—the mind of the observer. Does he imagine that the mind of the observer has nothing to do with the conclusion? Does he consider it merely as a blank sheet of paper? Has it not, on the contrary, a complex constitution of its own,

which modifies the facts observed, as the constitution of the stomach modifies the elements of the
food, which it converts into blood ?   Would a
lunatic, an idiot, or an inferior animal, draw the
same conclusions from the facts of life, as a sane
and normally constituted mind ?   If not, then he
must explain the normally constituted mind, *before*
he is justified in making a single observation.
But the truth is, his explanation of the mind *follows*
his observations, because it is deduced from them.
It is clear, therefore, that he has been *assuming* the
mind in every step which he has taken to *explain*
the mind, which is unphilosophical and absurd.

Emerson sees this absurdity, and resigns all
hope of *explaining* the Mind.   His only alternative
is to take his stand on the Mind, and account for
Nature.   Like Carlyle, he regards Nature as existing to represent Mind—as the vast *symbol* and
hieroglyph of Mind.   This view falls into accord
with our natural intuitions ; and commends itself
alike to the man-of-the-world, the poet, and the
religious thinker.   What interest, for example,
could there be in the actions, sayings, manners, and
behaviour of men, but that they are the *signs* of
thought and character ? And what is this but the
admission, that the outer and visible is the *symbol*
of the inner and invisible ?   What charm could
mere sensuous beauty have for us, but that it *refers*
to that inner sea of Beauty, of which it is the mani-

festation ? The fact, too, that we use the objects and appearances of Nature as *language* to express our thoughts and feelings is another proof of how naturally we regard the World as the *symbol* of Mind.

'Every word,' says Emerson, 'which is used to express a moral or intellectual fact, if traced to its root, is found to be borrowed from some material appearance. *Right* means *straight* ; *wrong* means *twisted*. *Spirit* primarily means *mind* ; *transgression* the crossing of a line ; *supercilious* the raising of the eyebrow. We say the *heart* to express emotion, the *head* to denote thought, and *thought* and *emotion* are words borrowed from sensible things and now appropriated to spiritual nature . . . Every appearance in Nature corresponds to some state of the mind, and that state of the mind can only be described by presenting that natural appearance as its picture. An enraged man is a lion, a cunning man is a fox, a firm man is a rock, a learned man is a torch. A lamb is innocence ; a snake is subtle spite ; flowers express to us the delicate affections. Light and darkness are our familiar expressions for knowledge and ignorance ; and heat for love. Visible distance behind and before us is respectively our image of memory and hope.'

The metaphors, too, which the poet employs to express the wide compass of human sentiment, ranging from the ordinary emotions of joy and sorrow, up to those ethereal tones that impinge at times on the very circumference of our being, are all combined from natural appearances. Unless the *spirit* of these appearances were identical with

the *spirit* of the poet's thought, his thought would
be unintelligible.   In parables and proverbs also
we have natural facts selected as *pictures* of moral
truths.   In such proverbs as ' Make hay while the
sun shines,' ' A rolling stone gathers no moss,' and
the like, the natural fact is of no significance whatever, except as the *expression* of a moral fact.

Emerson, perceiving that Nature is the symbol
of Mind, is led by the very gravitation of thought
to that *Cause of causes* that works in, through, and
behind all things.   Indeed, to lead us up to that
transcendent Being is the last and highest end of
Nature, as to feed and clothe us is its first and
lowest.   If we survey the economy of the World
from an elevated standpoint, we shall find that it
works everywhere for Beauty, Goodness, and Justice.   But to see this, we must fix our eye on results, not on processes and means.   A healthy
balance is kept between animal and vegetable life,
although the animal aggrandises itself at the expense of the plant ; between the different races
of animals, although accomplished by a round of
ferocity and antagonism, race preying on race ;
between the different activities of human beings,
although each individual would impose on his
fellows his own way of thinking, and, if he had the
power, would fashion the world in his own image.
In all this, we see that Nature works, not for the
exclusive benefit of any *one* creature, but for the

Good of *all* ; for broad and even-handed Justice ;
and amid all her complexities struggles everywhere
up into Beauty. ' The spirit and peculiarity,' says
Emerson, ' of that impression which Nature makes
on us is this, that it does not exist to any one or
to any number of particular ends, but to numberless
and endless benefit ; that there is in it no private
will, no rebel leaf or limb, but the whole is oppressed
by one superincumbent tendency.' This respect
for the *whole* in the disposal and distribution of
parts, is the direct inworking of that Divine Cause,
which, by its omnipresence, overpowers the self-will
of individuals, and reduces every refractory atom
into subservience to its own ends. The Universal
Spirit pervades every particle, and constrains every
clod, every crystal, every plant, every animal, and
every man, so that none can rebel. All private
eccentricities are rounded in by that mighty arc, as
the irregularities of the earth's surface, by the curve
of the sphere.

Is this view of the World whimsical and arbitrary ? Or, is it, on the contrary, founded on a
principle so universal and inherent, that it cannot
be evaded or denied ? It is founded on the fact
of Polarity. Every particle is armed with two
opposite poles. The result is, that there is a self-
poise in the whole and in every part ; and any excess of direction in animal or plant that would
disturb the universal harmony, is at once counter-

balanced. 'The World,' says Emerson, 'looks
like a multiplication-table or a mathematical equa
tion, which, turn it how you will, balances itself.'
He has abundantly illustrated this in his essay on
Compensation. The earliest appearance of these
two poles is in Matter itself, which physicists
are obliged to conceive as consisting of centres
of force, which attract and repel each other
at the same time. Indeed, the Evolutionists (as
I shall point out in my next Essay) deduce the
endless variety of the World from a *fixed* quantity
of force, which is made up of these antagonistic
forces of *attraction* and *repulsion*. But what we
have here to observe is, that these two poles are to
be met with everywhere ; in centrifugal and centripetal gravity ; in electricity and magnetism ; in ebb
and flow of waters ; in heat and cold ; in chemical
affinity ; in rhythm of motion and of sound ; in inspiration and expiration ; in male and female.
' An inevitable dualism bisects Nature, so that each
thing is a half, and suggests another thing to make
it whole, as mind, matter ; man, woman ; odd,
even ; subjective, objective ; in, out ; upper, under ;
motion, rest ; yea, nay.' In mechanics, what is
gained in power, is lost in time, and *vice versâ.* In
the animal kingdom, no creatures are favourites, but
every advantage is compensated by a defect. The
same creature pays for an excess of development
in one part, by a reduction in another. If the

head and neck are large, the trunk and extremities
are small. The same law is seen in the relation
that exists between the soil and climate of a
country, and the character of the men who inhabit
it. The fertility of the tropics tends to enervate
the character ; the comparative sterility of the
temperate zone, to strengthen it. The same compensation. insinuates itself into the administration
of nations. 'If the government is cruel, the
governor's life is not safe. If the taxes are exorbitant, the revenue will be defrauded. If the
criminal laws are too sanguinary, juries will not
convict. If the law is too mild, private vengeance
comes in.' In commerce, as we all know, the
cheapest are often the dearest commodities, as the
cheapest is often the dearest labour. In the human
mind the same law reappears.

'The ingenuity of man,' says Emerson, 'has always been
dedicated to the solution of one problem—how to detach
the sensual sweet, the sensual strong, the sensual bright,
&c., from the moral sweet, the moral deep, the moral fair ;
that is, again, to contrive to cut clean off this upper surface so thin as to leave it bottomless ; to get a *one end*
without an *other end*. The soul says, Eat ; the body
would feast. The soul says, the man and woman should
be one flesh and one soul ; the body would join the
flesh only. The soul says, Have dominion over all
things to the ends of virtue ; the body would have the
power over things to its own ends . . . Men seek to be
great, they would have office, wealth, power and fame.
They think that to be great is to possess one side of

nature—the sweet without the other side—the bitter. This dividing and detaching is steadily counteracted. Pleasure is taken out of pleasant things, profit out of profitable things, power out of strong things, as soon as we seek to separate them from the whole. We can no more halve things and get the sensual good by itself, than we can get an inside that shall have no outside, or a light without a shadow.'

Vanity, in its attempt to make a good impression, defeats itself. The man who borrows cannot rid himself of the tormenting sense of obligation. Pride is dearly purchased at the expense of the sentiments and heart. Truth is sacrificed where bigotry, intolerance, and prejudice are cherished. When we do a mean action, or an injury to our fellow-man, we loose our erectness of character. The guilty are haunted by remorse, or, if they escape it by hardening themselves, it is because they have lost their manhood, and have sunk in the scale of being.

The great ends of Goodness, Justice, Beauty, and Truth are thus everywhere accomplished by the *same* means, carried successively up to higher and higher platforms. It is this Unity of Idea that gives every object its *universal* character ; so that the meanest blade of grass is a mirror of the Universe. ' The true doctrine of omnipresence,' says Emerson, ' is that God reappears with all his parts in every moss and cobweb. The value of the Universe contrives to throw itself into every point.

If the good is there, so is the evil; if the affinity, so the repulsion; if the force, so the limitation.' 'Although no diligence can rebuild the Universe in a model by the best accumulation or disposition of details, yet does the world reappear in miniature in every event, so that all the laws of Nature may be read in the smallest fact. For this reason a mercury or index of intellectual proficiency is the perception of identity.' It is owing to this pervading Unity, that Nature always leaves on the poetic mind a harmonious impression. To this Unity is due also the universality which we attribute to great works of Art. As each individual object or event has its *roots* in the universal, it may be so represented as to be a perfect picture of human life. Hence a drama of Shakspeare, a song of Burns, a sonata of Mozart, or a picture of Raphael, is intelligible alike to the meanest and the most cultured understandings.

'Not only resemblances exist,' says Emerson, 'in things whose analogy is obvious, as when we detect the type of the human hand in the flipper of the fossil saurus, but also in objects where there is great superficial unlikeness. Thus architecture is called 'frozen music' by De Stael and Goethe. Vitruvius thought an architect should be a musician. 'A Gothic church,' said Coleridge, 'is a petrified religion.' Michael Angelo maintained that to an architect a knowledge of anatomy is essential. In Haydn's oratorios, the notes present to the imagination not only motions as of the snake, the stag, and the

elephant, but colours also, as the green grass. The law
of harmonic sounds reappears in the harmonic colours.
The granite is differenced in its laws only by the more or
less of heat from the river that wears it away. The river
as it flows resembles the air that flows over it; the air
resembles the light which traverses it with more subtle
currents; the light resembles the heat which rides with it
through space. Each creature is only a modification of
the other; the likeness is more than the difference, and
the radical law is one and the same. A rule of one art
or a law of one organisation holds true throughout
Nature. So intimate is this Unity that, it is easily seen,
it lies under the undermost garment of Nature and be-
trays its source in Universal Spirit. For it pervades
Thought also. Every universal truth which we express
in words implies or supposes every other truth. *Omne
verum vero consonat.* It is like a great circle on a sphere
comprising all possible circles; which, however, may be
drawn and comprise it in like manner. Every such
truth is the absolute *Ens* seen from one side. But it
has innumerable sides.'

Justice, Beauty, Goodness, and Truth are, as I
have said, the ultimate *ends* of Nature. We have
already seen this exemplified in the equity and
balance that adjusts the conflicting forces of the
animal and vegetable kingdoms; in that 'golden
mean' which cannot be overstepped without in-
stant compensation—that moderation which cannot
be abused without ruinous recoil. But it is seen,
dynamically, also, in the gradual amelioration
which the planet has undergone, from the earliest

geological epoch up to the present time. There has been an advance not only in intelligence, but also in order, justice, and beauty. In the primeval world, order and justice are seen working their way darkly, through the polarity of unconscious molecules, and the struggles of rival races; but when we arrive at Man, these high attributes have become purer and more concentrated, and have emerged into *consciousness.* The megatheria and ichthyosauri of the older epochs are the first rough blockings of the marble, which in later periods is chiselled into a more finished beauty. Nature eventually succeeds in throwing off her quadruped disguises, and clothes herself in a human form of such compactness, mobility, and transparency, that the workings of the spirit may be seen through it. And, finally, in the highest order of men, the spirit is, as it were, set free altogether, and seeks anew to create for itself a fairer, purer, and better world. The artist, for example, after drinking in the beauty of Nature's works, reproduces on the canvas an ideal beauty which ' never was on sea or land.' The poet, too, following the spirit of Nature, carries her flowing tendencies a little farther, and anticipates that perfection which she is struggling to attain, through a tough, unyielding medium. The philanthropist, moved by the miseries of mankind, tries to leave the world a legacy of benefits, free from the cruelty and inhumanity with which they are purchased among the primitive races, and even now, too often, among ourselves.

But the most incontestable proof that these high attributes of the Soul are the *ends* of Nature is, that, whereas all other gifts and benefits have their penalties and compensations, there is no tax on justice, goodness, and truth. With every increase of virtue, we are conscious of having *ascended* a step in the scale of existence. The good man, the wise man, the just man, is the height of humanity. He shares the nature and attributes of the First Cause, and is therefore superior to the ebb and flow of circumstance. The world has borne witness to this in every age, by the devotion with which it has followed, and even worshipped, those who have conquered Fate, or who have sacrificed their lives for principle, for virtue, for humanity.

This mode of representing the World, by its harmony with the native intuitions of the mind, carries with it the highest certificate of truth, and, while congenial to the poet and religious thinker, is based on the most rigid inductions of experience.

From Emerson's *insight* into the World follow as a consequence his *religion* and *ethics*. The steadfastness of our faith is, in the long run, proportioned to the clearness and sureness of our intellectual perception. Insight is the root out of which springs faith as the flower. As long as a man's diagram of the Universe is not incredible, that is to say, as long as it is not contradicted by positive knowledge, authority and tradition are sufficient to keep alive the flame of faith. But when Science and criticism have forced its main positions, faith begins to waver, and disruption and collapse gradually ensue. For a time, especially during seasons of religious excitement, the fervour of imagination may suffuse the old formulæ with a deceptive appearance of vitality, but this soon passes away, and disintegration sets in. But Emerson's religion requires no such exercitations of the imagination to vivify it. It rests on an insight into Nature so comprehensive and central, and yet, withal, so subtle and delicate, as to defy the last revelations of the scalpel or microscope. He sees evidence on all sides of an Omnipresent Being, working steadily for Justice, Goodness, and Truth. His first great *duty*, therefore, is as clear as the sun. It is *Self-Renunciation*—the disregard of Self in the ardour to forward these great ends. This is no new truth. It is as old as the world, and has been unconsciously believed and followed by the army of noble men who have in all ages dedicated their lives to virtue ; although it was first distinctly announced and inculcated by the Christian Religion. From whatever point of view we regard the facts of life, this truth steps at once into the foreground as our first moral duty. If we look at the

World in perspective, and represent to ourselves the moving panorama of life as it comes up from the past, we see it working steadily towards greater intelligence, goodness, and justice. Our first duty, therefore, is to assist this deliberate tendency by a voluntary and spontaneous obedience. We, too, must choose and forward the just, the good, the true ; and this demands, at every turn, the subordination of our personal and selfish inclinations, or, in a word, Self-Renunciation.

If, on the other hand, we prefer to look at the world of the present, we shall find running through it two groups of tendencies. The first group ministers to the welfare of the *individual*, and comprises the appetites, ferocities, propensities, and natural weapons of offence and defence. The second group ministers to the welfare of the *whole*, and includes the spiritual and moral laws of Man. That the former of these two groups of tendencies must be subordinated to the latter, is supported by an appeal either to the facts of consciousness, or to the facts of Nature. Consciousness testifies that the moral and spiritual are higher and nobler than the individual and selfish impulses, and that when any antagonism arises the latter must yield. The facts of Nature equally teach us that the *individual* is always sacrificed to the *general* welfare. The myriads of insects that come into being, flutter for a moment, and are extinguished ; the inexhaustible productiveness of lower organisms, serving as prey for enemies, a few only surviving to continue the species ; the prodigality of seed and blossom, and paucity of fruit ; the internecine warfare of races—all prove how little Nature regards individuals, and how readily she sacrifices them to higher ends. Or, again (slightly varying the mode of representation), if we regard Nature as made up of individual objects and creatures, none of which are independent and unrelated, but all attached to, and *dependent* on the Supreme Will at the centre of things ; our first duty is still dependence and trust, and our highest good a lowly obedience and Renunciation.

Emerson is deeply imbued with this truth. ' The man,' he says, ' who renounces himself comes to himself' He would have us take our egotism and nothingness out of the path of the Divine circuits. A voluntary obedience he regards as the last lesson of life —as the choral song that rises from all created beings.

Without Renunciation, Action must ever be incomplete, and wanting in purity and beauty. As long as we are under the dominion of vanity, avarice, or fear, we are only half men, and everything we do is alloyed. The men who have deeply moved the world, and have become its ideals, have been lifted out of themselves by some intense enthusiasm, some burning Idea, which has smelted the dross out of their natures in its consuming heat, or converted it into fiery energy, and so has left them free to act with the momentum of natural forces.

If Action without Self-Renunciation is incomplete, so is Self-Renunciation without Action. Our beliefs, to be sound and wholesome, must be con tinually reinforced by practical activity ; otherwise they are sure to degenerate into passivity and sen timentalism, and soon become noxious. The efforts we make to realise our convictions in life and con duct, may be fairly taken as an index of their strength and genuineness. The world hates discursiveness, but honours those who can concentrate the resources of their mind on a point, whether it be a work of art, a speech, a poem, a campaign, or an invention. But the necessity of putting our principles into practice is now so generally acknowledged, that it needs little enforcing. It could only have been prominently brought forward as a set-off against the remnant of asceticism still clinging to the popular teaching. Emerson thinks that the scholar cannot, for the sake of his nervesa nd his nap, afford to lose any action in which he can partici pate, for it brings a rich return of wisdom, and loads his words with power. Only so much do we truly know, as we have lived. But he has no superstition about it. While, on the one hand, he sees that Action strengthens belief and intensifies it ; on the other, he sees that it narrows the mind. While he sees that it converts doubt into certainty, and in the labyrinths of opinion and logic, determines the point on which the issue depends ; he sees also that it imprisons us in a limited circle of ideas. He would not have the scholar sacrifice any wider principle of activity in deference to the popular modes. Epaminondas was a man of action ; but he thinks that if Epaminondas were the man he takes him for, he would have been content to sit still, if his lot had been his. There can be no doubt that the work a man is engaged in, stamps its im press on the mind, and soon begins to tell on his body, face, and manners. The routine of the labourer, the mechanic, the soldier, the tradesman, the lawyer, does not tend to form complete and harmonious characters. Nor does the work of the man of science, who is engrossed in details. Hence the necessity of Culture, to correct this excess of bias and partiality, and to bring all the faculties and sides of our nature up to rotundity. To approximate in any measure to a complete and universal manhood, Action and Contemplation must alternate, in accordance with that deepest law of Nature—the Law of Polarity, whereby out of the action and reaction of two opposite principles springs the harmonious whole.

We come now to Emerson's mode of representing the Human Mind. Like Carlyle, Emerson

holds the doctrine that the intellectual and moral
faculties act and react on each other, and form an
organic unity. He sees the hopelessness of analy-
tical metaphysics, and the impossibility of treating
the Mind under any one division of its activity,
whether intellectual, moral, or practical ; because
sincerity and *earnestness* are the parents of intellectual *perception*, and intellectual perception is the
parent of *action*. They pass rapidly into one another,
like pictures in a dissolving view. He sees that the
interdependence between intellect and morals is so
intimate, that *talent* uniformly sinks with *character.*
He sees that of two men of equal practical activity,
the one whose *thought* is deepest is the strongest *character.* He sees, in fine, that the really simple-minded
have the key to all the virtues and talents, as they are
in the spirit which contains them all.   ‘ Those who
are capable,’ says he, ‘ of humanity, of justice, of
love, of aspiration, stand already on a platform
which commands the sciences and arts, speech and
poetry, action and grace.   For whoso dwells in this
moral beatitude, already anticipates those special
powers which men prize so highly.’

Emerson also holds the doctrine (discussed at
length in the preceding essay) that we are led by
the Imagination. ‘ I find men,’ says he, ‘ the vic-
tims of illusion in all parts of life. Children, youths,
adults, and old men are all led by one bauble or
another.’   In his essay on *Illusion* he has illus-

trated this by examples in great abundance : the
boy whose fancy is captivated by the exploits of
heroes ; the children in the desolate hovel, who,
nevertheless, hung it round with romance, like the
children of the happiest fortune ; the prosy alder-
man, who imitates the air and actions of those he
admires, pays a debt quicker to the rich than to
the poor, wishes for the bow and compliment of
some leader in the State and in society, and
dies all the happier ; and the scholar who is the
victim of every new book. 'Life,' says he, 'is a
succession of lessons which must be lived to be
understood. All is riddle, and the key to a riddle
is another riddle. There are as many pillows of
illusion as flakes in a snowstorm. We wake from
one dream into another dream. The toys, to be
sure, are various, and are graduated in refinement
to the quality of the dupe. The intellectual man
requires a fine bait ; the sots are easily amused.
But everybody is drugged with his own frenzy.'

Up to this point the views of Emerson and
Carlyle are, at bottom, the same. Their modes of
representing the World and the Human Mind are,
in the main, substantially alike. But when they
proceed to apply their principles to the practical
affairs of life, they begin to diverge, and ultimately
end as far apart as the poles. The remaining pages
will be devoted to a consideration of the causes of

K

this divergence, and its effects on their literary and political views.

Men may be regarded in two aspects—either as to their common likeness, or their individual differences. The fundamental elements of the human mind, like those of the body, are the same in all. Not only are the appetites and passions the same, but also the spiritual, moral, and intellectual attributes. But Goodness, Justice, Truth, and Beauty, are also sides of the Divine Mind, and are the ends to which Nature works. All men, therefore, in virtue of a common possession, have equal access to the mind of God, and the secrets of Nature. This identity is the basis of the *equality* of men.

Men are not only like one another, but, on the other hand, each is unlike every other. No two are precisely alike physically ; no two are precisely alike mentally. These differences are due to what is called organisation or temperament. One man is sensitive and nervous, another is dull and phlegmatic. One is more susceptible to truth, another to beauty, another to goodness. In one, the passions are so strong, that the voice of reason is but faintly heard ; in another, selfishness is so exorbitant, that nobility and generosity of nature are starved and attenuated. The diversity is as endless as the combinations of every faculty, in every quality and degree. This diversity is the basis of the *inequality* of men.

The stern fact of *organisation*, on the one hand, and on the other, the *identity of nature* (by virtue of all men having within them the attributes of the Spirit which made the World), are recognised alike by both Carlyle and Emerson. During a course of lectures which Emerson delivered on the *Conduct of Life*, it was complained that in discoursing on Fate, Wealth, and Power, he had attributed so much influence to organisation and temperament, that he had run the risk of abolishing the Godlike from human affairs altogether. He replied that there was no danger of his falling into his ink-pot ; that he had no lack of belief, and could afford to give a long line to scepticism, in the assurance that a grain of Faith, like a grain of mustard seed, could uplift a mountain of Fate. He then proceeded to discourse on Worship, Culture, and Beauty, as the antagonism and counterpoise to Fate, Wealth, and Power.

Carlyle also recognises that all men are equally open to divine illumination and power, by virtue of an identical nature. The remark of Novalis that 'bending before Man is a reverence done to this Revelation in the flesh,' he quotes frequently and with approval. Doctor Johnson, he remarks, would only bow to a clergyman or man with a shovel hat. He would go farther, and would bow to any man whatever, whether he had a hat or not ; because every man has within him the Godlike. When he

remembered, however, that there was also a personal and selfish side to Man's nature, he confessed
that the bow had better be withheld, lest it should
be pocketed by Vanity.   His doctrine, that the intellectual depends on the moral, and that men
choose to be little, because they will not sweep
from their hearts insincerity, cant, and intolerance,
proves also how clearly he perceives that all men
have equal access to the Divine Spirit, if they would
but suffer themselves to be guided by it.

But when Emerson and Carlyle proceed to
apply their principles to practice, they at once take
different sides.   Emerson takes his stand on the
Godlike in Man ; Carlyle on temperament and or
ganisation.   This divergence affects their whole
literary procedure, and characterises their views
of Man, History, Art, Biography, and Politics.   It
first makes its appearance in their views of the
relationship that should exist between man and
man.   Carlyle, taking his stand on *organisation*,
preaches Hero-Worship ; Emerson, taking his
stand on the *Godlike*, preaches Self-reliance.   Let
us trace briefly the chain of thought that leads up
to these respective conclusions.

Carlyle sees a Divine Will behind the everchanging phenomena of the World, as clearly as he
sees a thinking principle like his own behind the
countenances of his fellow-men.   He sees also that
our greatest good is in obedience to this Will, as

revealed in the physical, organic, and spiritual laws. But as these lie in a web, intricate and involved, there is great difficulty in reading and understanding them. Among the mass of men, however, there appear from time to time, individuals gifted with the rare insight which enables them to interpret these laws, and make them known to their fellows. In olden times these were the prophets and law-givers whom the nations have so willingly followed— Menu, Moses, Solon, Lycurgus, Mahomet. For, although all men may be equally open to the Divine Mind, by virtue of a common nature, there is practically this immense difference between them. We have experience every day of the fact that one man is more richly gifted than another. And such is the intimate interdependence of insight and morality, that the truly intellectual man is also the truly just, the truly good, the truly magnanimous man ; as the sincere and earnest man is the man of solid judgment also. The Great Man is therefore the highest present exponent of the Divine Will. All the attributes of God are represented in him in miniature—justice, goodness, truth. It follows accordingly that in reverencing the Great Man, and following his guidance, we are practically manifesting our belief in God, and our desire to obey His commandments. Hence Carlyle's remark that ' all religion issues in due practical Hero-worship.' Besides, in following those whom we believe to be our superiors, we are obeying one of the deepest instincts of our nature. Let a number of men (to take a hypothetical case), all equally independent and unrelated, meet together and form a society. Let each have a fair opportunity of demonstrating his powers and capacity to the rest; gradually the society loses its homogeneous character, mystic fibres shoot through it in all directions, and the whole becomes bound together into an organic unity. It has become a hierarchy, with the ablest man at the top. Thenceforward the leader gives guidance and protection in return for loyalty and obedience. He becomes, accordingly, the Ideal after which the whole society fashions itself. His manners, tastes, aspirations, and culture are imitated. Each member tries to realise in himself the virtues he so much admires; and insensibly, through the magnetic influence of a single man, the whole society has been elevated and refined; and at the same time, every faculty and side of the nature has been duly and becomingly exercised. This is precisely what we should expect. Men are made better, not by stuffing their minds with dead and barren abstractions, which jingle through the head and never touch the heart; but by elevating before them a living, concrete, human Ideal, which, by the hold it takes on the Imagination, warms the heart, stimulates the will, incites emulation, and draws out the active powers. 'Of this thing be certain,' says

Carlyle, 'wouldst thou plant for Eternity, then plant into the deep, infinite faculties of man, his Fantasy and Heart; wouldst thou plant for Year and Day, then plant into his shallow, superficial faculties, his Self-love and Arithmetical Understanding, what will grow there.'

This train of thought is the key to Carlyle's views of the present state of Society. We have lost, he thinks, our Religion, and practical belief in God has faded into a faint and incredible tradition. Duty has, in consequence, almost lost its divine meaning, and is resolved into the diluted form of 'enlightened self-interest.' Having lost our belief in God, we have lost with it our sense of Human Worth. Our governors have become impotent, and unworthy to govern ; we have become free, and are unwilling to obey. Loyalty has accordingly died out, and the ties that formerly bound Society together have become so relaxed, that 'Cash-payment is now the sole nexus between man and man.' For guidance, we have 'laissez-faire' and 'Supply and Demand'; for obedience, we have insubordination and 'independence.' Society is fast becoming an aggregate of conflicting atoms, without any principle of coheslon to keep it from falling to pieces. What, then, is to be done? 'Universal Suffrage' and 'the Ballot-box' can do nothing for us. Our votes will only reflect ourselves, and our false and unworthy admirations. They will never return the Great Man to the helm of affairs, but rather the sham-great man. As the loss of our religion was the primary cause of our unhappy condition, our first step must be to find it again. We must come again to realise that there is a God presiding over the affairs of this World, and not Mammon or the Devil. Then, and not till then, will Religion cease to be an empty grimace, Duty an empty name. Human worth will again be recognised and exalted ; human baseness, cast down and execrated. Man will again unite himself to man ; a religious loyalty will spring up in our hearts ; and Society, like the human body, with all its members in mutual relation and subordination, will become a healthy, vital, indivisible unity. But in his impatience with the present, Carlyle has become reactionary, and casts longing glances at the past. He is so disgusted with our present ' state of anarchy,' that, if he cannot have the natural despotism of genius and virtue, he will put up with, and even welcome, a despotism of force. He lays so much stress on order, that he would sacrifice to it, conscience, aspiration, sentiment, freedom, the healthy diversity of thought and character. He would have the drill-sergeant in every parish, and every household ; and would convert the world into a barracks. He would gag the press, enslave the negro, and have mankind driven like a flock of sheep. He prefers ignorance, with the stupid docility of the peasant, to knowledge, with its liability to ambition, restlessness, and in-subordination. Let us now turn to Emerson.

Like Carlyle, he believes in God, and sees that our highest freedom and blessedness lie in a cheer ful submission to His will. But taking his stand on the Godlike in man, he will allow of no inter-preter of that will, but the individual reason and conscience. If we listen, in all humility, to the voice of truth within ourselves, we shall hear the right word. There is no need that we should take either our beliefs or our duties from any man. It is true that there are differences of gifts among men. It is true that the moral and intellectual faculties are commensurate with each other. But no single in-dividual has the full complement of virtue, and, therefore, of talent. Temperament and organisation interfere at every turn. If a man's genius is com-manding, his active powers are apt to be torpid or paralytic ; if he has promptness and energy, his range of sight is apt to be contracted. So that, although the unity of the moral and intellectual is a true law, it is, like every law, rather a tendency than a realised fact. It is so thwarted by organi-sation, that if we expect to find it in any particular person, we are likely to be disappointed. Society is not, therefore, as Carlyle imagines, a hierarchy, where talent and virtue *united*, rise in an ascending scale ; on the contrary, talent and virtue are rather delegated to individuals in *parts*, so that it takes

the whole society to give us the fulness and pro
portion we want. Even the greatest men are but
fragments. 'A man,' says Emerson, 'is like a bit of
Labrador spar, which has no lustre as you turn it in
your hand, until you come to a particular angle,
then it shows deep and beautiful colours. There is
no adaptation or universal applicability in men,
but each has his special talent, and the mastery of
successful men consists in keeping themselves
where and when that turn shall oftenest be prac-
tised.' The reason why we attribute to some men
a completeness and harmony of nature, is, because,
by a well-known trick of the imagination, we as-
cribe universality and completeness, to whatever we
regard with love and admiration. Or, as Emerson
has it, 'on seeing the smallest arc we complete
the circle.' We meet with a man, for example,
distinguished for some special trait of brilliancy or
utility, which takes our fancy. We imagine that
the whole figure is of the same proportion as that
one member. But we shall discover our error, if
we place him in circumstances requiring a different
order of faculty. Then we shall see his limitations;
and when we do, it is all over with him. For the
Infinite which is in every man, demands for its
satisfaction, objects and attributes that are eternal
and inexhaustible. There can be no doubt that
reverence for great men is one of the deepest instincts of our nature. It is, therefore, natural, just,

and reasonable, that we should, in all humility, give reverence where reverence is due. But the service that even the greatest men can render us is but temporary and prospective. If our minds are expansive, we soon outgrow them. We drain them, one after another, like cisterns. Unless we are to be the slave of a puerile delusion, we can surrender heart and soul to no man. It is true, also, that living Human Ideals lead us and stimulate us more than any other ; but like the toys of children, they are to be cast aside when they are outgrown. The only Ideal which we can worship with our whole soul, and on which we can rest for ever, is that great Power, which casts up men like pebbles from the infinite deep—that Sea of Light, of whose unexplored splendour man is but an exhalation. If then, every man, no matter how brilliant or profound, is but a fragment, a partialist, let us stand on our own feet, look at the facts of life for ourselves, in all honesty and sincerity, and we shall see the truth that concerns us, as well as another.

With Emerson, this virtue of Self-reliance includes all the virtues, and he never loses an opportunity of enforcing it. He regards it as the basis of all character, as the essence of all heroism. The great men whom we so much admire, differ from ourselves, chiefly in this, that while we rely on them, they rely on themselves. To the literary man Self-reliance is indispensable. ‘Meek young

men,' says he, 'grow up in libraries, believing it to
be their duty to accept the views which Cicero,
which Locke, which Bacon, have given ; forgetting
that Cicero, Locke, and Bacon, were but young
men in libraries when they wrote these books.'
So little self-reliance is there in the masses of men,
that they are spoken of as 'the herd ;' and their
circle of thought and action can be predicted as
easily as the return of morning and night. It is
this imbecility of the masses that 'invites the im-
pudence of power,' and perpetuates slavery and
despotism. But Self-reliance, by breaking up the
torpid routine of thought, lets new light into the
darkened mind, and sets the world spinning on
the paths of progress. If, therefore, Hero-worship
has been the practical creed of the past, Self-
reliance is to be that of the future. But so closely
does every virtue lie to a corresponding vice, that
it is apt to fall into it. Self-reliance as easily de
generates into conceit and bombast, as Hero-wor
ship does into flunkeyism and meanness of spirit.
Still, by releasing men from their stupid idolatries,
and opening up to them the essential riches of
their own natures, it communicates hope, stimulates
aspiration, and gives new interest and value to life.

Emerson, accordingly, would put as little re-
straint as possible on the individual will. He admires the simplicity of Nature. The apple falls
when it is ripe. The planets fall in their orbits.

The walking of man and of all animals is a falling forward. Let us imitate this wise simplicity, and in all our actions follow the laws of our nature, without affectation or hypocrisy. Our spontaneous acts are the most beautiful and virtuous. Each man has a natural principle of selection, in his books, his studies, his employments, his amusements, his food. Let us not interfere with these unconscious instincts. Let us encourage every variety of talent and utility. Let each do his own work, and let his talent be the call. Coercion vitiates the moral nature. An iron uniformity would crush the fairest flowers of the mind, and would rob society of its richest and most delicate natures. He compares our ponderous State-machinery to the Roman aqueducts, which were laboriously constructed over hill and dale, but which were superseded when we discovered the simple law that water would always find its own level. He sees, of course, that the form of government in any country is the reflex of the prevailing culture ; and that, where men are ignorant, brutal, and selfish, there must always be a government of force. But, looking to the future, rather than to the past, he would open up to men full and unimpeded liberty, in the sublime faith that every evil as it arises will be checked by the natural reactions and compensations of their condition. He has no fear of Liberty, but invites us to it, as to a breath of morning after a long and troubled night. He sees that person and property will always have their due influence, whatever be the form of government. And as sure as every atom has two poles, so surely will any excess of force in one direction, generate a countervailing force in the opposite. Radicalism begets Conservatism; Conservatism, Radicalism. 'Wild liberty breeds iron conscience; the want of liberty, by strengthening law and decorum, stupefies conscience.' Where positive laws are few, custom supplies their place. Hence the less government, the better; the fewer laws, the better. Let each man do his own work, and his influence will, in the long run, be proportioned to the depth of his thought. His virtues will be measured by his actions, as a tree by its fruit. What we want is Character. That is the end of all edu cation, of all institutions, of all government. When that is formed, the State is no longer necessary. The upright man needs no policeman. As yet, however, we rely not on principle, but on men, on money, on organisation, on party. Let us now try the influence of Love. 'I think *that* the soul of Reform—the conviction that not sensualism, not slavery, not war, not imprisonment, not even government are needed, but in lieu of them all, reliance on the sentiment of man which will work best the more it is trusted.'

The literary procedure of Carlyle and Emerson

is marked by the same divergence which characterises their views on Society.

Carlyle's first concern was to extricate himself
from the perplexities and contradictions of life, and
to get, if possible, a sight of Deity at first hand.
Accordingly, in the *Sartor Resartus*, we find him
looking fixedly at phenomena until they become
transparent with their causes, and at these causes
until they fade and melt into Deity. We see
him stripping off, one by one, the successive ves-
tures which conceal, and yet reveal, the Eternal.
And having beheld the Divine Essence face to face,
as it were, he deems it his noblest mission to return
to the world, and try to conform men to the Divine
nature. His choice of means for this end is di
rected by his insight into human life. He believes
that the majority of men are incapable by themselves of unravelling the contradictions of Time ;
and of seeing God through the clouds and obscura
tions of sense. He sees that they are led by sensuous symbols which appeal to the Imagination.
And as he is convinced that the clearest symbols
of God are the lives of Great Men, he would accord
ingly hold these up as exemplars for their imita
tion and guidance. Hence he has spent the greater
part of his life writing History and Biography.
And as he thinks that in Action alone can greatness of mind attain its fulness and completion, he
prefers to select his heroes from men of action—

statesmen, warriors, kings. But Biography, to
have its full influence, must be a record of fact,
not a mixture of fact and fiction. He has therefore
spared himself no trouble to obtain access to accurate and reliable information. He tells us of the
weary hours he has spent, searching among mountains of rubbish for a grain or two of solid reality.
When his materials are collected, they do not lie
around him in distracted, amorphous heaps ; but
immediately begin to organise themselves. He
shoots a ray of genius through them, and the darkness becomes light. He breathes on the dry bones
and they become alive. The most widely-sundered
and apparently unrelated incidents are brought
together, and united, by subtle spiritual links, as
parts of an organic unity, to the deep laws of the
human heart. His biographies, in turn, illustrate
and enforce his cardinal principles of thought. In
his literary portraits, he points out with great truth
and penetration, that any limitation of *moral* sympathy is sternly compensated by a corresponding
limitation of *intellectual* power. But in his portraits of men of action, he labours under greater
difficulties. The morality of some of his heroes,
judged by conventional standards, is extremely
questionable ; and yet the facts are stubborn, and
not to be evaded. He cannot, like the poet and
writer of fiction, conform his incidents to the harmony of **his** picture. His only alternative, there-

fore, is to seize firmly the spirit of the character, and treat the obnoxious facts as superficial, casual, or non-essential. He accordingly throws the conventional morality to the winds, and sticks boldly to the essential and radical virtues of justice, veracity, and sincerity. He passes over the delinquencies of his heroes, with a light and easy censure, and sometimes, even, converts them into positive virtues. The brutality of Friedrich Wilhelm, the sensuality of Mirabeau, the corruption of Danton, the cold and flippant scepticism of Frederick the Great, instead of being condemned, are palliated. The sensitive reader is surprised and shocked, and the influence of these magnificent studies, so profound and full of genius, is, in consequence, somewhat impaired.

His treatment of History is equally original. He protested against the attempts of historians to press history into a particular theory. He saw that the times of Charlemagne and Luther were as full of life and colour, as to-day, and, that the motives of men *then*, were as mixed and incalculable as *now*. He would, therefore, endeavour, for his own part, to give as far as possible an accurate account of the real events, and leave the reader to draw his own theory. He knew that if he were successful, his pictures would illustrate as many different theories, as a living thing has sides from which it may be regarded. In the history of

the French Revolution, accordingly, he lifts the
curtain that veils the past, and lets us see for ourselves what was going on at a particular section of
time. By a series of vivid pictures, he shows us
what men were saying and doing, and thereby
enables us to realise what they were thinking and
feeling. We see, on the eve of the Revolution, the
corruption of the Court ; the convicted impotence
and falsehood of the Government ; and the distress
and starvation of the people. When the crisis
arrives and the drama is unfolding, the successive
acts are as incalculable, and can be as little foreseen, as the impulses of a mob. He accordingly
throws away all philosophical theories, all remote
causes, and connects the series of events with those
immediate impulses of the human heart that lead
directly to action—Hunger, ' Preternatural Suspicion,' Enthusiasm of Liberty, Vanity, Frenzy, and
Revenge.

Emerson, too, regards the Deity as the highest
and noblest object of human contemplation. When
he looks at Nature, and sees her everywhere bris-
tling with the polarity that ranges the meanest
trifle on the line of the Divine thought, he would
wonder and worship for ever. Carlyle, as we have
seen, would lead us up to God through the worship
of Great Men. But Emerson will allow no person,
however transcendent, to intercept the passage of
the Divine rays, and tinge their purity with sen-

suous colours. He would have us mount with him
to Deity through ascending circles of thought.
Hence he writes Philosophy. It is true that in
his *Representative Men,* he discourses on persons ;
but they are chiefly eminent philosophers. He
hastens over the details of their personal history ;
but delights to dwell on the great thoughts in which
they lived, and by which they climbed up the
ladder of Being to the First Cause. When he in-
dulges in incident, it is to illustrate by a pointed
anecdote the *spirit* of their thinking. Men are interesting to him, not as creatures of flesh and blood,
but in so far only as they are mouthpieces of Divine
wisdom. He is on his guard against a *personal*
influence. He sees how apt we are to fancy that
things done by men of 'position' or reputation, are
better than the same things done by plain people.
But with him, the measure and worth of any action
is the spirit from which it proceeds, not who did
it. Nor is he to be caught by the mere bulk and
uproar of a transaction ; but insists on judging it
by the depth of thought from which it emanated.
For the greatest action may be the most simple
and private concern. He admires Buonaparte, not
because he dazzled the vulgar eye, but because he
finds his maxims have that universal application
which characterises the master. He can translate,
he says, all his tactics into all his own. Carlyle
would elevate Great Men into standing ideals for

the world's worship, on account of the hold they
take on the heart and imagination, and the consequent elevation and aspiration they impart to
masses of men. Emerson, on the contrary, considers that the worship of great men degenerates
into superstition, that it introduces the worship of
personality, so that the most ordinary actions become sacred. He would, therefore, substitute for
it, a thought of the mind—an immortal Truth,
which, by breaking up these illusions of the heart
and imagination, would open up new modes of
thought, and compel the nations to march on the
road of progress. He would have such truths sink
into the mind, and ferment there, until they had
revolutionised the character and life Hence in
dealing with persons, instead of biographical pictures, he gives us spiritual delineations. In representing a man, Carlyle searches for the cardinal
impulse, and when he finds it, he makes it the
central point, around which the whole character is
organised. In Burns, it is sincerity ; in Johnson,
veracity ; in Voltaire, adroitness. Emerson, on the
contrary, composes his representation out of innumerable fragments, each of which corresponds to
some side or aspect of the mind. These are so closely
and finely inlaid as to form a perfect mosaic ; the
selection of the whole being controlled by the most
profound and piercing insight.

Carlyle is so enamoured of truth that he dis

parages all attempts to draw ideal characters after the just laws of the imagination. He admires Shakspeare more for his historical pictures than for his great constructive dramas. But it is questionable, whether there is not as much illusion, or, in other words, fiction, in the best biography as there is in ' Hamlet ' or ' Lear.' At all events, the point is worth raising for a moment. To begin with, no man can be raised out of his natural surroundings and isolated, without the imagination weaving around him mystic and fictitious attributes. If he is virtuous, he appears more virtuous ; if vicious, more vicious, by isolation. The very language, too, which describes a character so isolated adds another layer of fiction. It is a coloured medium, which stains every object that passes through it. It carries with it associations which it cannot shake off, and which adhere to the subject of the narrative. It is much the same with Art. A man's portrait makes a deeper impression on us when seen on the wall, than the man himself does when seen in a crowd. The poor beggar girl in the picture draws our sympathies and tears, but the original from which the picture was taken, stands shivering at the street-corner, cold and neglected. We are all the fools of these tricks of the imagination, and it is the office of literature to point them out, instead of perpetuating them, as it was the office of astronomy to dissipate the fictions associated

with the heavenly bodies. One of our most distinguished historians has affirmed, that the Science
of History consists, in separating, as far as possible,
the fiction from the truth in bygone transactions.
Accordingly, the legends of the saints, and the
ecclesiastical miracles of the early centuries are now
almost entirely discredited. We have yet to go a
step further, and strip off the fictions which still
adhere to persons and classes, and which so power
fully affect the true relations that should exist between man and man. We have yet to open up to
men the sense of that original identity which biography, art, history, and fame, do so much to
weaken or obliterate.

The object of biography, as ' a work of art,' is to
exhibit a man's inner life, by a record of the experiences which befell him. Every man has an
original cast of mind, which modifies the circumstances he comes in contact with, and which, in
turn, is modified by them. But no inventory of
the *circumstances* can furnish us with the key we
want. We may know the daily life and pursuits of
a friend. We may be able to form a fair idea of
the thoughts that are agitating him. We may
have shared, in confidence, his aspirations, hopes,
and perplexities. But the greatness, which makes
a man's genius or character worth recording, will
elude the most searching analysis. Who of Shakspeare's companions could have told us how he

came by his immense knowledge of life ? Who of
Buonaparte's comrades could have explained his
practical sagacity ? The truth is, thought and character, like a coral reef, are formed by the incessant
iteration of minute and trivial circumstances ; by
the imperceptible influence of those around us ; by
casual remarks in books, which excite new trains of
thought ; by the words or actions of obscure men,
who little thought they were rendering us an essential service, and were conveying a truth that would
go far to remodel our lives. A record of these
would be as tedious and prolix as Pepys ; and would
be inadmissible in ' a work of art,' where perspective
is so essential. There can be no doubt that, in
actual life, there are wide degrees of greatness and
meanness. But the greatest man is great, only in
high and rare moments ; the rest of his life is the
sober grey of ordinary mortals. By selecting these
eminent experiences and making them the staple
of a biography, we may produce an ideal, but not
a true picture. The biographer, in order to heighten
the interest of his narrative, and make it readable,
is justified, like the dramatist, in omitting the mean
and prosy details, and in selecting and linking together the bright and poetic circumstances. But if
he asks us to accept the record as the whole truth,
and holds it up before us as a Scripture to influence
and direct opinion, we must repudiate it.

Biographies are interesting, but they serve, after

all, for amusement and curiosity, rather than instruction. They teach no great or even new truth.
They illustrate the rewards of virtue, perseverance,
and the like ; or some wise saw, which is either so
trite, or so irrelevant, as to be without appreciable
influence on our own conduct. Each new day that
dawns on us brings with it new and unknown circumstances, and requires new and untried methods
to meet them. What was said or done in other
days, and under other circumstances, by great men,
is of little service to us. Nothing will avail but insight into the conditions we work under, into the
connections of causes, and the course of events.
We want a new thought, not a new picture. I have
read scores of books for curiosity or pleasure, but
only the general truths that I have gleaned on the
way have been of use to me. The great masters of
thought enrich us with deep and wide principles,
which we can test on the open arena of the world,
and apply to the shifting circumstances of every
day. They plough the mind into furrows of
thought, break up the soil, and plant truths that
will bear fruit to all time.

Biographies are good as stimulants. It is, perhaps, the best service they render us. They fan
the emotions, and rouse us in despondency by the
traditions of heroism and virtue. But unless they
plant deep and solid truths, their effects are as
evanescent and transitory, as the billows which the

wind drives over the surface of the waters. There is no danger that knowledge should destroy our reverence for great men, or prevent our doing our duty to our fellows. On the contrary, what is most wanted, especially at the present time, is an insight that will clear up our contradictions and perplexi ties, and enable us to see *what* is to be reverenced, and *what* is to be done. When the weeds that entangle and impede us are cut away, we may rest in the sure faith that religion, reverence, and duty, will spring up in human hearts, as naturally and spontaneously as love.

Emerson participates in Carlyle's reaction against those who saw in History only a reflection of their own theories. But at the same time, he sees that no history can be more than an approximation to the actual reality. Preconceived opinions are in- terwoven with the narrative. The picture is coloured and distorted by prejudice. The merest fragment of what occurred is reported. Motives are mixed, and cannot be separated. The important elements are often so unobtrusive as to escape notice. The dust and uproar hide the real connection of events, and confound the judgment of the onlooker. The successive 'estimates' of different historians only replace one illusion by another. Hence he will not bury himself in dreary catacombs, among the dust of the dead, searching for what, when found, is not worth the trouble. He prefers to live in the sun-

shine of the day that is passing over him, which is,
as good as the days of Cromwell or Charles the
Fifth, and contains the same mingled elements—
the good and the evil, the greatness and meanness,
the happiness and misery, the hope and disappointment. He would study well the lessons *it* teaches,
and thereby supersede the use of history. ' Be lord
of a day,' says he, ' by wisdom and virtue, and you
may put up your history books.' Our own life is
the only reliable historical record. In proportion
as that has been wide, deep, and varied, is our
ability to interpret the ages that are past. A deep
insight into the life that was passing around him,
and a sympathy with every phase of it, enabled
Goethe to reproduce the antique world. Although
human nature is the same in all ages, certain *ideas*
or principles have more influence at one period than
at another. In one age, it is valour, or physical superiority : in another, it is asceticism, or chivalry, or
liberty. We can live over in ourselves these dominant ideas, as we do the common human nature.
We can realise the particular thoughts or feelings
which gave rise to these particular forms of society.
We can interpret the youth of the world from our
own youth, its past from our past. We can understand its Fetishism, its Polytheism, its Monotheism.
We have the private key to its Theological, its Metaphysical, its Positive stages. Each new experience
of our own throws light on what great masses of

men have done. 'Every revolution,' says Emerson,
'was first a thought in one man's mind, and when
the same thought shall occur to another man it is
the key to that era. Every reform was first a
private opinion, and when it shall be a private
opinion again, it will solve the problem of the age.
The fact narrated must correspond to something in
me to be credible or intelligible.' We can understand the Puritans from certain passages in our
own experience. Why then spend our lives in endeavouring to unearth the details of their history?
If we have not had their experience, no catalogue
of their actions or opinions will enable us to *understand* it. Either way, therefore, it is a matter of
indifference. 'This life of ours is stuck round with
Egypt, Greece, Gaul, England, War, Colonisation,
Church, Court, and Commerce, as with so many
flowers and wild ornaments, grave and gay. I will
not make more account of them. I believe in
Eternity. I can find Greece, Asia, Italy, Spain,
and the Islands—the genius and creative principle
of each and all eras in my own mind.'

From what has been said, the reader will
already have anticipated the wide divergence between Carlyle and Emerson, in their views of Art.
Carlyle would have the artist give us the literal
facts, as they alone form a sure basis for belief, and
therefore, for effective example. The Lives of Great
Men, being, in his opinion, the clearest and surest

revelations of the Godlike, are accordingly the highest works of Art. Emerson, on the contrary, would have the artist give us the *soul* of the facts; creation, not imitation; the spirit and splendour, not the prose and details. But fixing his eyes on the overflowing Cause that streams through Nature, he makes little of any man's life, or of any piece of human art. The genius that created 'Hamlet' and 'Othello' could go on producing the like until the end of time. A picture more or less is of little consequence. Instead of filling the world with commentaries on these magnificent productions, let us strive, each for himself, to get a little of that insight from which 'Hamlet' and 'Othello' flowed as easy and natural effects.

HERBERT SPENCER.

I PROPOSE in this essay to examine Mr. Herbert Spencer's theory of the Universe. For this purpose I have selected his book on 'First Principles,' as it contains the germs of that system of Philosophy, which in subsequent volumes he has developed with such breadth and fulness of detail. I do not intend following Mr. Spencer through the mass of scientific facts which illustrate rather than establish his principles, but prefer to fix the attention of the reader on those cardinal points on which his whole system turns, and hope by a careful selection of quotations, so to light up the central principle, that its scope and significance may be clearly seen. It is perhaps unnecessary to say that the very keystone of his philosophy is his doctrine of the 'Persistence of Force.' With this, every minor doctrine is tuned into harmony, and from it every subsidiary principle takes its cue and emphasis. Every road leads to it, and its dependencies link it with the circumference and extremities of his 'System of Philosophy.' But that

the reader may see in what way this central doc
trine is established, and also that my criticism may
be rendered more intelligible, I have deemed it
expedient, without further preliminary, to give a
brief, rapid sketch of the book itself.

Mr. Spencer opens by remarking, that as there
'is a soul of goodness in things evil,' so there is a
soul of truth in things erroneous. Beliefs that
have met with a wide acceptance among men have
generally a germ of truth in them ; and if these
beliefs are antagonistic, the common ground between them, in all probability, contains that germ.
If we let discordant opinions cancel each other,
what remains, being that in which they all agree,
may be accepted as the truth. Now, of all antag-
onisms of belief, the oldest, widest, deepest, and
most important is that between Science and Religion. Is it not possible, then, that if we could
discover the truth that is common to both, it would
form the basis of a permanent reconciliation between them ? With this object in view, he proceeds
first to examine the essential conceptions involved
in the different orders of religious belief By the
necessities of our mental constitution, we are bound
to ask ourselves the origin of this Universe into
which we are born. Only three possible answers
can be given, which correspond respectively to the
Atheistic, Pantheistic, and Theistic theories. It
must either be self-existent, self-created, or created

by an external agency. But on examination neither of these theories is thinkable or conceivable. It cannot be self-existent, because that implies existence without a beginning, which is inconceivable. It cannot have been self-created, because that would involve that existence, having remained for some time in one form, has passed into another form without a cause, which is also inconceivable. Nor can it have been the result of an external agency, as it is impossible to conceive where the matter out of which it is created could have come from, and really implies the creation of matter out of nothing.

If we turn from the *origin* to the *nature* of the Universe, we are met with like difficulties. From the nature of our intelligence, we are bound to assume a Cause for the effects produced on our consciousness — the sensations of form, colour, sound, the various attributes of bodies, &c. If we assume a Cause, it commits us to a First Cause. This First Cause cannot be finite, else there were an Infinite *uncaused* outside of it. It cannot be dependent, else that on which it depends would be the First Cause. It is therefore both Infinite and Absolute. And yet these three conceptions, the Cause, Infinite, and Absolute, when viewed in conjunction as attributes of the same Being, are contradictory; for the Cause as such cannot be Absolute, as it is related to its effect, nor can the Absolute as

such be a Cause. Besides, if it were a Cause, it|
could not be Infinite, as it would be limited by its
effect. Thus all theories as to the nature and
origin of the Universe, are inconceivable and unthinkable. But it is to be observed that while they
all disagree in their special interpretations, they all
agree that the Universe is a mystery ever pressing
for interpretation. And 'if Science and Religion
are to be reconciled, it must be on this deepest,
widest, and most certain of all facts—that the
Power which the Universe manifests to us is
utterly inscrutable.'

Mr. Spencer now turns to examine ultimate
Scientific ideas. All Science deals with the relations in Time and Space, of Matter, Motion, and
Force. But what are Time and Space? One hypothesis is, that they exist outside of us ; another
is, that they exist internally and are connected in
some way with our consciousness. If they exist
outside of us, they cannot be non-entities ; nor can
they be attributes, as there is nothing of which we
can conceive them to be attributes ; nor, like attributes, can we think of them disappearing, even if
everything else disappeared. They must be entities then. But they cannot be entities, as they
have no attributes ; nor like entities can we assert
of them either limitation, or absence of limitation.
On the other hand, they cannot be connected with
our consciousness, for consciousness testifies to their

existence outside, not inside the mind. Space and
Time, then, are wholly incomprehensible. Next, as
to Matter. We cannot conceive it to be infinitely
divisible, for it would take infinite time to follow
out its divisions ; nor can we conceive a particle so
small as not to admit of further division. It cannot
be absolutely solid, else it would not be compres-
sible. Nor can it consist of solid units not in contact, but acting on each other by attractive and
repulsive forces, as the same difficulties would
attend the constitution of the units. The hypothesis that it consists of centres of force without
dimensions, which attract and repel each other in
such a way as to be kept at specific distances apart,
is also untenable, for it is impossible to conceive
force residing in points occupying no space whatever. Matter, then, like Time and Space, is absolutely incomprehensible. Again, as to Motion.
We cannot get rid of the idea that there are points
in Space, with respect to which all motions are absolute, and yet, on the other hand, in unlimited
space, motion is inconceivable, because place itself
is inconceivable. The *transfer* of motion, too, how
is it effected ? The striking body has not com
municated to the body struck, a thing, nor has it
communicated an attribute. What then has it
communicated ? Force, too, is incomprehensible.
On lifting a chair, the force we exert is equal to the
weight of the chair, and we cannot conceive it as

equal without being *like* in kind, since equality is conceivable only between things that are of the same nature. And yet to imagine this, is to endow the chair with consciousness, which is absurd. Again, how are we to understand the connection between Force and Matter? Matter is known to us only through its manifestation of Force; our ultimate test of Matter being the ability to resist. And yet, on the other hand, resistance is equally unthinkable apart from Matter—from something extended. Again, it is impossible for either extended or unextended 'centres of force' to attract and repel one another without the intermediation of some sort of matter; and even if we assume an ethereal medium (which must have interspaces between its particles), we are bound to think that Matter acts on Matter through absolutely vacant space—a conclusion which is absolutely unthink able. The exercise of Force, then, is altogether unintelligible.

Mr. Spencer now turns to the internal world— the world of consciousness—and finds that the belief in our own personality cannot be got rid of. But the mental act in which self is known, implies, like every other mental act, an object perceived and a perceiving subject. If the object perceived is self, what is the subject that perceives? or if it is the real self that thinks, what other self can be thought of? Thus the personality of which we are all con-

scious, cannot be really known at all. Ultimate
Scientific ideas, then, like ultimate religious ideas,
are in their substance and genesis quite incomprehensible.

This inability of knowing the real or *Absolute*
nature of things, leads Mr. Spencer to the conclusion that all knowledge is of the *Relative* only.
This conclusion he finds confirmed on considering
the nature of our intelligence. An object to be
known must be classed as of this or that kind. A
bird, for example, is said to be known, when it can
be referred to this or that order or species. A fact
to be understood must be included in a wider generalisation. The falling of a stone, for example,
is said to be understood, when it is referred to the
Law of Gravitation. Obviously, then, the widest
class, or widest generalisation, not being included
in any other, cannot be *known*. Knowledge, too,
implies likeness as well as difference. To be known,
a thing must not only be distinguished from some
other thing, but must also be like something else.
But the First Cause, the Infinite, the Absolute,
cannot be like anything of which we have sensible
experience ; it cannot, therefore, be known. Again,
Life itself is merely the adjustment of inner actions
to meet certain outer actions ; as, for instance, the
adjustment of the muscles, which keep us erect, to
meet the attraction of gravitation, ever tending to
draw us down. Intelligence, too, even the highest,

is simply the adjustment of our ideas to meet the complexities of the World around us—is only the relation between our minds and the World, and gives, therefore, no insight into the *things* between which the relation exists.

All knowledge, then, being of the *Relative* only, what shall we say of the *Absolute*—of that which transcends knowledge? Does it exist? Is it a Reality? Mr. Spencer replies in the affirmative. To say that we do not know the Absolute, is to imply that the Absolute exists. We are conscious of the Relative as existence under conditions and limits ; the abstraction of these conditions and limits still leaves something that filled up their outlines, and this indefinite something constitutes our consciousness of the Absolute.

Here, then, is the basis of that reconciliation between Science and Religion which we set out to seek. Common Sense asserts the existence of a Reality ; Objective Science proves that that Reality cannot be what we think it ; Subjective Science shows why we cannot think of it as it is, and yet we are compelled to think of it as existing; and in this assertion of a Reality utterly inscrutable in nature, Religion finds an assertion essentially coinciding with her own. We are obliged to regard every phenomenon as a manifestation of some Power by which we are acted upon. Though Omnipresence is unthinkable, yet as experience discloses no bounds to the diffusion of phenomena, we are unable to think of limits to the presence of this Power, while the criticisms of Science teach us that this Power is incomprehensible. And this

consciousness of an incomprehensible Power, called
Omnipresent from inability to assign its limits, is just that
consciousness on which Religion dwells.

I may here remark, without anticipating the
argument, that this incomprehensible Power, or
Absolute Reality, which reconciles Religion and
Science, turns out to be the ' *Persistence of Force.*'

Mr. Spencer now proceeds to the second division of his subject—the Knowable—and asks, first,
what is Philosophy ? After showing that it com-
prehends and consolidates the highest generalisations of Science, he defines it to be *completely
unified* knowledge. But before taking a first step
in the rational interpretation of things, certain fundamental intuitions, which are essential to the process of thinking, must be assumed as true ; leaving
the assumption of their truth to be justified by the
results, *i.e.*, by ascertaining that all the conclusions
deducible from the assumption correspond to the
facts as directly observed. The first assumption
is that a *likeness* or *difference* exists when con
sciousness testifies to it. The second is the assertion of a likeness and difference transcending all
other, viz., that of *self* and *not-self*, or of *subject*
and *object*. But besides these divisions of the manifestations of the Unknowable into *self* and *not-
self*, there are certain modes in which the manifestations cohere, and are invariably presented to us.
These modes are *Matter* and *Motion*, as presented

to us in *Space* and *Time.* Of course we can deal
with Matter, Motion, Space, and Time as realities,
although they are only *manifestations* of the Unknown Reality. For the test of Reality is *persistence* in consciousness, and under the conditions
of our constitution, they are as persistent as the
Unknown Reality could be, were it present in
thought. Now, although Matter, Motion, Time,
and Space are apparently all necessary data of
intelligence, yet analysis shows that they are built
up of, or abstracted from, experiences of *Force,*
through the resistance offered to our muscular
energies ; while Force itself is derived from nothing
else, as it can be interpreted in terms of nothing
else. But before Science and Philosophy can begin,
we must recognise further the truth of *the Indestructibility of Matter* ; for if, instead of having to
deal with *fixed* quantities and weights, we had to
deal with quantities and weights which were apt
wholly or in part to be annihilated, there would be
introduced an incalculable element fatal to all positive conclusions. So, too, with the *Continuity of
Motion.* These truths are shown to follow from
the very nature of thought. Thought consists in
the establishment of relations. There can be no relation established, and therefore no thought framed,
when one of the related terms is absent from consciousness. Hence it is impossible to think of
something becoming nothing. But, besides this,

the doctrines of the Indestructibility of Matter and Continuity of Motion are supported by scientific experiment. If we burn a candle slowly away, the weight of the resulting carbonic acid and water is found to be exactly equal to the weight of the candle, plus the amount of oxygen which has combined with it. We test it by weight, *i.e.*, by the amount of gravitative force it exerts. We *assume*, observe, that the attractive force of the earth *does not vary.* This is an important assumption, and leads Mr. Spencer to his doctrine of the 'Persistence of Force,'—the fact *that the quantity of Force in the Universe is fixed.* On what ground, he asks, do we assert the Persistence of Force? There can only be two kinds of proof. One is from our own sensation of it, but that does not persist. The other is from the Indestructibility of Matter and Continuity of Motion; but we have just seen that they are valid only on the assumption that Force is persistent. We have to assume the Persistence of Force to prove *them*; we cannot, therefore, assume them to prove the Persistence of Force. Obviously, then, the Persistence of Force is a truth of which no inductive proof is possible. It must be taken for granted. Indeed, we might be certain that there must be some principle, which, as being the *basis* of Science, cannot be established *by* Science. This principle, which transcends demonstration, is the Persistence of Force. Mr. Spencer next asks, *what* the Force is, of which we assert persistence? His reply is most important, and I must ask the reader to bear it in mind, as I shall have to consider it more fully farther on. He says it is that *Unknown Cause*, of which the phenomena of the World are but the *manifestations*; is that *Absolute Power* in which Religion and Science are reconciled.

On this doctrine of the Persistence of Force, as a groundwork, Mr. Spencer proceeds to build up his Philosophy of Evolution. The first corollary which he draws from the Persistence of Force, is the '*persistence of relations among forces*,' or what is commonly known as the *Uniformity of Law*. This truth is usually supposed to have been the slow result of experience; but Mr. Spencer points out that it is really strictly deducible from the Persistence of Force. I shall not give his proof here, as I shall have to quote it, in full, farther on. The next deduction drawn from the Persistence of Force is the doctrine of *the Transformation and Equivalence of Forces*, *i.e.*, that forces which seem to be lost, are transformed into their equivalents of other forces; or that forces which make their appearance, do so by the disappearance of pre-existent equivalent forces. This is illustrated by the motions of the heavenly bodies, by the changes going on over the earth's surface, by organic and super-organic actions. Mr. Spencer points out that the truth of the doctrine does not depend on the evidence he brings forward ; and adds that it *must* be true, as a *necessary corollary* of the Persistence of Force.   So, too, with the Law that '*Force follows the line of least resistance, or of greatest traction, or the resultant of the two,*' which is illustrated with great copiousness from the motions of planets round their axes and around the sun, from atmospheric currents, evaporation and condensation, organic growth, ' natural selection,' nervous discharges, and the direction of trade ; and which he asserts to be a *necessary corollary* from the Persistence of Force. The next truth he enunciates is, that *all motion is rhythmical* ; illustrated with equal abundance of detail from the motion of double stars, periodicities of planets and comets, day and night, magnetic variations, rains and droughts, beating of the heart, dancing, music, poetry, alternation of belief and unbelief in religion, &c. ; and like the others a *necessary deduction* from the Persistence of Force.

Now, these truths—the Indestructibility of Matter, Continuity of Motion, Transformation and Equivalence of Forces, Force following the line of least resistance, Rhythm of Motion—are co-extensive with all the sciences, and of the highest generality.   They are, therefore, of the character required to build up a Philosophy.   But they express only the laws of the separate factors, not of how they are combined to produce the World as we know it. We want a law that will formulate the changes actually passed through by all existence— by the Universe as a whole, and by every part ; as seen in the formation of the solar system out of nebulous matter, in the growth of animals and vegetables, from their germs through their successive stages, in the increase of Societies, and in the progress of Languages, Sciences, and Arts. That law Mr. Spencer finds to be the *Law of Evolution,* and defines it as '*an integration of Matter, and concomitant dissipation of Motion, during which the matter passes from an indefinite, incoherent homogeneity, to a definite, coherent heterogeneity, and during which the retained Motion undergoes a parallel transformation.*' This law holds true of all existences whatever. But we fall short of that *unified knowledge* which constitutes Philosophy, unless we know *why* it holds true of all existences. We must deduce it from some first principle. We saw that the Laws of 'the Transformation and Equivalence of Forces,' 'Force following the line of least resistance,' 'Rhythm of Motion,' were deducible from the Persistence of Force. If we can also deduce the Law of Evolution from the Persistence of Force, all knowledge will be unified, and Philosophy will have reached its goal. Mr. Spencer proceeds to show that it is so deducible. But as Evolution goes on in every part *simultaneously* with the Evolution of the whole, the transformations are so complex, that it is difficult to grasp the whole process at once. It may be broken into its factors, however, and each of these will be seen to be deducible from the Persistence of Force. What are these factors? They are '*the Instability of the Homogeneous,*' or the fact that any finite homogeneous aggregate must lose its homogeneity through the unequal exposure of its parts to surrounding forces; the '*Multiplication of Effects,*' or the increase of the complexity into which the homogeneous lapses by the action and interaction of the parts on one another, which produces the immense *variety* of the World; '*Segregation,*' or the clustering of the like, and separation of the unlike parts under the action of forces capable of moving them—which produces the *definiteness* and *individuality* of things; 'Equilibration,' or the balancing of all the forces, as they are successively met by antagonistic forces,—which produces the *harmony* everywhere seen throughout Nature. Mr. Spencer has illustrated each of these laws (which follow from strictly *mechanical* principles), with his usual wealth, by the facts of astronomy; by the formations on the earth's crust; by the structure of organisms; by the nature of man and phenomena of societies. He also asserts (and I shall examine the grounds of his assertion presently), that each of these laws is deducible from

the Persistence of Force.   As these separate
changes are only different aspects of one transformation, Evolution in general, and in detail,
becomes a *corollary* of the Persistence of Force,
and Philosophy has reached its goal.

From this slight sketch it will be at once
apparent, that the pivot on which Mr. Spencer's
philosophy turns is his doctrine of *the Persistence
of Force.*   It is this which gives unity to his
system.   It is this which is the *basis* of Science,—
the Law of Evolution being a *necessary* corollary
from it.   It is this which is the *object* of Religion,
being that Absolute Power of which the Universe
is only a manifestation.   It is this, therefore, which
is the common ground of *reconciliation* between
Religion and Science.

Now, I shall endeavour in the following pages
to show, firstly, that the Persistence of Force is *not*
the basis of Science; and that the Law of Evolution
is *not* a corollary from it; secondly. that it is *not*
the Absolute Power of which the Universe is a
manifestation; and that it is *not* the object of
religious worship.

Let us then determine, from Mr. Spencer's own
account, whether the Law of Evolution follows of
necessity as a corollary from the Persistence of
Force.   The factors which we have seen go to
make up the *Law of Evolution* are, when considered separately, the '*Uniformity of Law*,' the

'*Equivalence and Transformation of Forces,*' '*Force following the line of least resistance, or of greatest traction, or their resultant* ;' and the '*Rhythm of Motion* ;' when considered in their combined action, are the '*Instability of the Homogeneous,*' the '*Multiplication of Effects,*' '*Segregation,*' and '*Equilibration.*' I shall examine each of these separately. To illustrate the Uniformity of Law, Mr Spencer says (§ 64)·

Let two equal bullets be projected with equal force ; then, in equal times, equal distances must be travelled by them. The assertion that one of them will describe an assigned space sooner than the other, though their initial momenta were alike, and they have been equally resisted (for if they are unequally resisted the antecedents differ), is an assertion that equal quantities of force have not done equal amounts of work, and this cannot be thought without thinking that some force has disappeared into nothing, or arisen out of nothing.'

Evidently here the Uniformity of Law follows from the fact that the *quantity* of Force in the Universe is *fixed*. With regard to the Transformation and Equivalence of Forces, he says (§ 73):

Each manifestation of Force can be interpreted only as the effect of some antecedent force ; no matter whether it be an inorganic action, an animal movement, a thought or a feeling. Either this must be conceded, or else it must be asserted that our successive states of consciousness are self-created. Either mental energies as well as bodily ones are quantitatively correlated to

certain energies expended in their production, and to
certain other energies which they initiate, or else nothing
must become something, and something must become
nothing.   The alternatives are to deny the Persistence of
Force, or to admit that every physical and psychical
change is generated by certain antecedent forces, and
that from given amounts of such forces, neither more
nor less of such physical and psychical changes can
result.

Clearly, the ' Transformation and Equivalence of
Forces' follows from that *fixed* quantity of Force
which constituted the Universe a moment ago, and
the transformations of which constitute the Universe of the present moment.

Again, in regard to the direction of Motion, Mr.
Spencer says (§ 75) :—

*From universally coexistent forces of attraction and re-
pulsion* there result certain laws of direction of all motion.
Where attractive forces alone are concerned, or rather are
alone appreciable, movement takes place in the direction
of their resultant, which may in a sense be called the
line of greatest traction.   Where repulsive forces alone
are concerned, or rather are alone appreciable, movement
takes places along their resultant, which is usually known
as the line of least resistance.   And where both attractive
and repulsive forces are concerned, or are appreciable,
movement takes place along the resultant of all the
tractions and resistances.   For (§ 81) to assert the contrary is to assert that a force can be expended without
effect—without generating an equivalent force ; and by
so implying that force can cease to exist, this involves a
denial of the Persistence of Force.

Again (§ 74) he says :

Matter cannot be conceived except as manifesting forces of *attraction* and *repulsion.*

Here, too, it is evident that the Law that 'Force follows the line of least resistance' is a corollary, not from the Persistence of Force, but from a *fixed quantity of Force made up of coexistent forces of attraction and repulsion.* And as Force which is made up of coexistent forces of attraction and repulsion is Matter, therefore the law really is a corollary from a *fixed quantity of Matter.* Take again the Rhythm of Motion. Mr. Spencer says (§ 88) :

It needs but to contemplate this action and reaction (of a tuning-fork pulled on one side by the finger) to see that it is, like every action and reaction, a consequent of the Persistence of Force. The force exerted by the finger in bending the prong cannot disappear. Under what form, then, does it exist? It exists under the form of that cohesive tension which it has generated among the particles. This cohesive tension cannot cease without an equivalent result. What is its equivalent result? The momentum generated in the prong while being carried back to its position of rest. This momentum, too— what becomes of it? It must either continue as momentum, or produce some correlative force of equal amount. It cannot continue as momentum, since change of place is resisted by the cohesion of the parts, and thus it gradually disappears by being transformed into tension among these parts. This is retransformed into the equivalent momentum, and so on continually.

But in the same section he says :—

Given the coexistence everywhere of antagonistic forces—a postulate which, as we have seen, is necessitated by the form of our experience—and Rhythm is an inevitable corollary from the Persistence of Forces.

It is clear from these quotations that the Rhythm of Motion is a corollary, *not ¹from the Persistence of Force, but ¹from coexistent antagonistic forces, fixed in their quantity* ; or, in other words, from a *fixed quantity of Matter.*

We come now to the factors which in their *combined* action constitute the Law of Evolution, and which are made up of the laws we have just considered. The first is the 'Instability of the Homogeneous.' Mr. Spencer says (§ 155) :—

One stable homogeneity is hypothetically possible. If centres of force absolutely uniform in their powers were diffused with absolute uniformity through unlimited space, they would remain in equilibrium. But all *finite* forms of the homogeneous—all forms of it which we can know or conceive—must inevitably lapse into heterogeneity. In three several ways does the Persistence of Force necessitate this. Setting external agencies aside, each unit of a homogeneous whole must be differently affected from any of the rest by the aggregate action of the rest upon it. The resultant force exercised by the aggregate on each unit being in no two cases alike both in amount and direction, and usually not in either, any incident force, even if uniform in amount and direction, cannot produce like effects on the units. And the various positions of the parts in relation to any incident force preventing them from receiving it in uniform amounts and directions, a further difference in the effects wrought on them is inevitably produced.

It is to be noticed here that the 'Instability of the Homogeneous,' and consequently the Law of Evolution, can only follow from a *finite* or *fixed* quantity of Force. And as this Force is made up of antagonistic forces of attraction and repulsion, it really follows from a *fixed quantity of Matter.* The 'Multiplication of Effects,' which is merely the complexity arising from the action and inter-action of the parts into which the homogeneous lapses, evidently follows from the same principle as the 'Instability of the Homogeneous,' and will not require further specification here. The same may be said, too, of 'Segregation,' which, in its most abstract form, Mr. Spencer says amounts to this (§ 169) ·

That in the action and reaction of force and matter, an unlikeness in either of the factors necessitates an unlikeness in the effects ; and that, in the absence of unlikeness in either of the factors, the effects must be alike, otherwise the differentiated force produces no effect, and force is not persistent.

It is scarcely necessary to remark that here, too, the Law of 'Segregation' follows not from the Persistence of Force, but simply from a *fixed quantity of Force or Matter.* In regard to 'Equilibration' Mr. Spencer says (§ 176) :—

'We have seen that phenomena are interpretable *only as the results of universally-coexistent forces of attraction and repulsion.*' But 'the forces of attraction and repulsion being universally coexistent, it follows that all motion is·motion under resistance. . . . The denser or rarer medium which occupies the places from moment to moment passed through by such moving body having to be expelled from them, as much motion is abstracted from the moving body as is given to the medium in expelling it from these places. This being the condition under which all motion occurs, two corollaries result. The first is that the deductions perpetually made by the communication of motion to the resisting medium cannot but bring the motion of the body to an end in a longer or shorter time. The second is that the motion of the body cannot cease until these deductions destroy it. In other words, movement must continue till equilibration takes place, and equilibration must eventually take place. Both these are manifest deductions from the Persistence of Force. To say that the whole or part of a body's motion can disappear save by transfer to something which resists its motion, is to say that the whole or part can disappear without effect ; which is to deny the Persistence of Force.'

Taking these quotations together, ' Equilibration ' follows clearly from a *fixed* quantity of Force made up of universally coexistent *forces of attraction and repulsion* ; and not from the Persistence of Force.

Thus the law of Evolution, on analysis, is found to be deducible, not from the Persistence of Force, but from a fixed quantity of force, made up of co-existent forces of attraction and repulsion. Had

Mr. Spencer so deduced it, he would have proceeded
on strictly scientific principles. But his system
would have lost that magnificence and harmony
which he triumphantly asks us to contemplate
from a distance where details are lost to view.
Those who may have supposed that by ' the Persistence of Force ' Mr. Spencer only meant that
*fixed quantity of Force made up of antagonistic
forces of attraction and repulsion,* will be surprised
when they learn what the force is of which he
asserts the Persistence. I shall quote in full. He
says (§ 60) :—

But now what is the force of which we predicate
persistence? It is not the force we are immediately
conscious of in our muscular efforts, for this does not
persist. As soon as an outstretched limb is relaxed the
sense of tension disappears. True, we assert that in the
stone thrown, or in the weight lifted, is exhibited the
effect of this muscular tension, and that the force which
has ceased to be present in our consciousness exists elsewhere. But it does not exist elsewhere under any form
cognisable by us. It was proved (§ 18) that though, on
raising an object from the ground, we are obliged to think
of its downward pull as equal and opposite to our upward pull ; and though it is impossible to represent
these pulls as equal without representing them as like in
kind, yet, since their likeness in kind would imply in the
object a sensation of muscular tension, which cannot be
ascribed to it, we are compelled to admit that force as it
exists out of our consciousness is not force as we know
it. Hence the force of which we assert persistence is

that *Absolute Force* of which we are indefinitely conscious as the necessary correlate of the Force we know.
Thus, by the Persistence of Force, we really mean the
Persistence of some Power which transcends our knowledge and conception.   The manifestations as occurring
either in ourselves or outside of us do not persist, but
that which persists is *the Unknown Cause of these manifestations.*   In other words, asserting the Persistence of
Force is but another mode of asserting an Unconditioned Reality, without beginning or end.   Thus, quite
unexpectedly, we come down once more to that ultimate
truth in which, as we saw, *Religion and Science coalesce.*
On examining the data underlying a rational theory of
phenomena, we find them all at last resolvable into that
datum without which consciousness was shown to be
impossible—the continued existence of an Unknowable,
as the necessary correlate of the Knowable.   Once commenced, the analysis of the truths taken for granted in
scientific inquiries inevitably brings us down to this
deepest truth, in which Common Sense and Philosophy
are reconciled.

We see here that by the Persistence of Force
Mr. Spencer means that *Absolute Force* of which
the forces of the Universe are but the *manifestations,* and which is the object of Religious worship,
as well as the basis of Science.   It is evident,
therefore, that he does not mean by it that fixed
quantity of Force, made up of co-existent forces of
attraction and repulsion, from which, by an examination of the above quotations, we have seen
Evolution to be really deducible.   For it is quite

absurd to suppose that a fixed quantity of force in antagonistic forms, or of Matter, constitutes that Absolute Reality which is the object of Religious worship. This leads me to the proof of my next point, viz., that the Persistence of Force is *not* Absolute, but Relative ; and is *not* the basis of Religion, or that in which Science and Religion are reconciled. That it is not Absolute will be seen on all hands. To begin with, Mr. Spencer expressly asserts (§ 176) that

the universally coexistent forces of attraction and repulsion are the *complementary* aspects of the Absolutely Persistent force.

But in § 74 he says ·

These universally co-existent forces of attraction and repulsion must not be taken as realities, but as our *symbols* of the Reality. They are the forms under which the workings of the Unknowable are cognisable by us— modes of the Unconditioned as presented under the conditions of our consciousness. But while knowing that the ideas thus generated are not *absolutely* true, we may surrender ourselves to them as *relatively* true.

Obviously, then, if these antagonistic forces of attraction and repulsion are only Relative realities, and if, at the same time, they are the *complementary* aspects of the force that is persistent, it follows that the Persistence of Force is a Relative, not an Absolute Reality. That the Persistence of Force is a Relative, and not an Absolute Reality, becomes evident on considering

Mr. Spencer's own account of the Theory of Evolution. This hypothesis proceeds on the assumption that Matter, existing originally in a diffuse homogeneous condition, passes through specific phases. and transformations, called Evolution, ending in dissolution. This dissolution by the forces it sets free, produces a return to the original homogeneous condition, which passes through the same phases and transformations, and ends as before ; the same process going on continually. These changes occur because the force is *fixed* in quantity, and is made up of *antagonistic* forces, which determine the direction of the motion. It is clear, then, that at any given point in the process, the transformations are the necessary results of the preceding conditions, or antecedents. Otherwise some force would be lost, and with Mr. Spencer this is to deny the Persistence of Force. The force, then, which persists is that original quantity of Force which remains always the same. The forces that constitute the Universe yesterday, are the causes of the forces that constitute the Universe to-day. But the Universe of to-day is Relative, therefore the Universe of yesterday is Relative. And, therefore, the Persistence of Force is *Relative*, and not *Absolute*. And here we may see that in Mr. Spencer's theory, and, indeed, in all scientific theories of the Universe, there is and can be no room for an Absolute Cause at all. If one cause is sufficient to account for a fact, it is absurd to assume a second. All scientific causes are merely antecedents. Mr. Spencer himself admits this. He says that 'the most conspicuous antecedents are causes, and the accompanying ones conditions.' If then we ask the cause of that original homogeneous condition of Matter which all theories of Evolution assume as the commencement of things, and are told, as we are by Mr. Spencer, that it is the effect of forces let loose in the dissolution of the preceding evolutionary cycle, where shall we find, or, indeed, where is the room for, an Absolute Cause at all ? That there is no room for it in Mr. Spencer's theory will be apparent on examining his attempt to find a place for it. He says (§ 26) ·

We are conscious of the Relative as existence under conditions and limits ; it is impossible that these condi tions and limits can be thought of apart from something to which they give the form ; the abstraction of these conditions ·and limits is by the hypothesis the abstraction of them only ; consequently there must be a residuary consciousness of something which filled up their outlines ; and this indefinite something constitutes our conscious ness of the Non-Relative, or Absolute.

Now, Time, Space, Matter, Motion, and Force constitute the Relative, and are known, as Mr. Spencer has elsewhere shown, through muscular sensation. If sensation is abolished, instead of being conscious of the Absolute, we are really conscious of nothing at all. If we abolish our eyesight, for example, which is the condition of our knowledge of the stars, we should so far be unconscious of their existence. To the senses there is and can be no general existence apart from the aggregate of special existences. And to abolish these special existences by taking away the limits and conditions under which they are known, instead of leaving us the Absolute, leaves us nothing at all. For the Absolute is that which lies *behind* Time, Space, Matter, Motion, and Force, and is the Cause of these phenomena. It is separated from them by the whole distance between the Creator and created. It is got, not by abolishing the limits and conditions of the Relative, but immediately from the intuition of Cause in the Mind. Without this intuition we should be, like the lower animals, unconscious of its existence.

In the meantime it is important to consider Mr. Spencer's reasons for supposing that the Persistence of Force is the Absolute Cause of things. The first is given in the extract I have quoted, where he contends that we cannot think of the force existing in a chair as equal and opposite to the force expended in lifting it, without its being like in nature. This would be to endow the chair with consciousness—with a sensation of muscular tension that cannot be ascribed to it. We are compelled, therefore, to admit that force as it

exists out of our consciousness, is not force as we
know it. Hence the force of which we assert
Persistence is the Absolute Force. Now, the fallacy in this is obvious. For the force is not in the
consciousness, but in the muscles. It is merely
known through consciousness. Consciousness itself
is known to us as existence only, and, although
connected with force, is not known as Force. If
the force in the muscles, then, is Relative, so must
be the force in the chair. The muscular force is
Relative, because it is a correlated force, and all
correlated forces are Relative, the conversion of
food into muscle equally with the conversion of
light into heat. Besides, both muscles and chair
have been evolved out of that original homogeneous condition of matter, and as it is Relative,
so must they be. Nor is Mr. Spencer more successful when he turns to investigate the nature of
our consciousness of the Persistence of Force, with
the view of strengthening his argument for its
being the Absolute Cause of things. He says
(§ 61):

The Unknown Power, of which neither beginning nor
end can be conceived, is present to us as that unshaped
material of consciousness which is shaped afresh in every
thought.

Now, all forms of consciousness have physical
forces as their physical sides. These forces are correlated, and like all correlated forces must be Relative.

The Unknown Power, then, which is present to us must be Relative, unless it be maintained that the unshaped material of consciousness has no physical counterpart.　But to assert this is to admit a form of consciousness independent of nervous action. As Mr. Spencer cannot do this without abdicating everything distinctive of his philosophy, we can only conclude that the Persistence of Force or Unknown Power is Relative.　He says also (§ 61) ·

The truth that Force is indestructible is the obverse of the truth, that the Unknown Cause of the changes going on in consciousness is indestructible.

We have seen above, that, with Scientific Thinkers, the cause of all changes lies in the antecedents of these changes.　The cause of the changes going on in consciousness must lie in antecedent states of consciousness.　Will Mr. Spencer assert that these states are indestructible?　If he objects that there is a continuous thread of consciousness, which is never broken, as far as we can know, I reply that this cannot be urged by one whose whole philosophy is framed on the assumption that there can be no form of consciousness which is not merely the expression of nervous changes; and to assert that nervous changes are indestructible is, of course, absurd.　In fact, all Force, persistent or other, *must* be Relative.　Were it Absolute, it could not be known as force.　Mr. Spencer has himself shown that the idea of force arises by successive experiences out of the resistances offered to our muscular sensation. But to be known through sensation is precisely what distinguishes the Relative from the Absolute. Whatever can be touched, seen, or in any way apprehended by the senses, is Relative. Mr. Spencer may attribute absoluteness to unknown *existence*, not to unknown *force*.

I shall now proceed to consider Mr. Spencer's next main doctrine, viz., that the Persistence of Force is the object of Religion, as well as the basis of Science, and is that in which they are reconciled. The promise Mr. Spencer holds out to earnest minds, of reconciling Religion and Science, has heightened the interest which his writings have inspired. The world is full of unbelief. A shallow scepticism has become fashionable, and is openly paraded. Science sits in high places, prescribing for the souls as well as the bodies of men. The present generation has drunk deeply, and a general unrest has settled on the most active spirits. The human mind, freighted with Materialism, has lost its poise. The tyranny of physical law has enchained and subjugated the soul. The cry for relief comes up ever and anon from some robust, unconquered mind, and, heard above the general wail, is the expression of the general need. For man requires a religious belief, to restore that equilibrium to the mind which scientific modes of thought have temporarily disturbed. It is therefore natural that anyone coming with truths, that will reconcile the aspirations of the heart with the teachings of experience, should be eagerly welcomed. And yet it is chiefly to this attempt to reconcile, by scientific methods, Religion and Science, that I trace Mr. Spencer's errors. His system of thought has been weakened by secret contradictions, and is found, when closely scrutinised, to be, at bottom, the old atheism that we know so well. For what common ground can there be between Religion and Science? They can only be reconciled by being kept apart. They lie on different planes, and are referred to different categories in the hierarchy of the mind. Science deals with the *relative*, Religion with the *absolute*. Science converses with the *forces of Nature* and elicits their hidden connections and interdependencies ; Religion, with that which lies *behind* these forces, and to which they all consentingly refer. In Science, everything is linked with what precedes and what follows. This thing refers to that, that to the next—an inextricable web, causes being only the most conspicuous antecedents. Religion presses beyond this moving procession of lustrous, everchanging phenomena, which has come down to us from unknown time, and goes on to unknown time, seeks a reason for the whole, and finds its home in the First Cause of all. They cannot be reconciled by Science. Science reduces the complex phenomena of the World into terms of Matter, Motion, and Force, and he would indeed be a skilful thaumaturgist who could get out of it more than Matter, Motion, and Force. Mr. Spencer's attempt to get out of it an object of worship, is, as I have said, the root of all his errors. That Science and Religion should harmonise, it was necessary that the Persistence of Force should be *absolute*. But I have already shown it to be *relative*. And having made the Persistence of Force the basis of Science, it was necessary for the unity and harmony of his system that it should be made also the object of Religion. To accomplish this feat was not easy, but Mr. Spencer's attempt has at least the merit of ingenuity. His plan is to represent two opposite and utterly distinct things under one term—the Persistence of Force. He attaches one meaning to it when he uses it as the basis of scientific truths, quite another when he uses it as the object of Religion. It is a curious fact that Mr. Spencer seems to have been quite conscious of this double position. For it is notice-able, that when he uses it as the groundwork of Science, he writes it in small letters ; when he uses it to represent the Absolute, the First Cause, he writes it in capital letters. The importance of this seemingly trifling circumstance will be seen, if we reverse the process, and write the Persistence of

Force with capital letters when it is the basis of Science, and with small letters when it is the object of Religion. To try and worship the merely natural forces would be equalled in absurdity only by attempting to deduce scientific truths from the First Cause alone. That Mr. Spencer uses the Persistence of Force in the two incompatible senses I have indicated, will now be shown. On examining his account of the Law of Evolution, and how it followed from the Persistence of Force, we saw that the Persistence of Force could only mean the *sum-total* of the forces of Nature, which (although undergoing endless metamorphoses) remain always the same in quantity. But when he makes it the object of Religion, he represents it as the *Cause* of these forces. Here are the quotations. In § 49 he says :—

'We have an indefinite consciousness of an Absolute Reality transcending relations [Persistence of Force], which is produced by the absolute persistence in us of something which survives all changes of relation. We have also a definite consciousness of relative reality [Time, Space, Matter, Motion, and Force] which unceasingly persists in us under one or other of its forms, and under each form so long as the conditions of presentation are fulfilled.'

Again, in the same section, he says: 'Reality under the forms of our consciousness [Time, Space, Matter, Motion, and Force] is but a conditioned *effect* of the Absolute Reality [Persistence of Force].'

He says again (§ 50) : 'Force, as we know it, can be regarded only as a certain conditioned *effect* of the

Unconditioned Cause [Persistence of Force]—as the relative reality indicating to us an Absolute Reality by which it is immediately produced.'

Again (§ 51), he enumerates the postulates which must be assumed before Philosophy can begin, as

'an Unknown Cause [Persistence of Force] of the known effects called phenomena, likenesses and differences among these known effects, and a segregation of the effects into Subject and Object.'

It is obvious, from the above quotations, that he uses the Persistence of Force as the *Cause* of the forces of Nature. Having, in one half of the book, used the Persistence of Force as simply the *sum-total* of the forces of Nature, in the other half he uses it as the *Cause* of these forces—that which lies behind them. I have not space at my disposal to point out all the contradictions which this double use of the Persistence of Force has led to. I shall mention here only one instance, and shall use it to prove that the Persistence of Force is not the object of Religion. In one of the quotations just given, Mr. Spencer says that both the Mind and the World are manifestations or effects of the unknown Cause. But in § 25 he says :

Life, in all its manifestations, including Intelligence in its highest forms, consists in the continuous adjustment of internal relations to external relations.

Whatever is in the mind must, then, be related to something in the world. The religious sentiment is in the mind. It must therefore have its object in the

world. But the World is only the *effect* or *manifes
tation* of the Unknown Cause. The object of Reli
gion cannot therefore be the Unknown Cause, or
Persistence of Force. If Mr. Spencer objects that
the Unknown Cause comes up into the World, and
also into the Mind, two alternatives are open to him.
Either the Unknown Cause, like everything else in
the mind, has its physical side in nervous changes,
or there is a form of mind not connected with nervous action. The first alternative is absurd ; the
second cannot be admitted by him except by renouncing, as I have said before, everything distinctive of his philosophy. The Persistence of Force,
then, cannot be the object of Religion. It has been
pointed out that it is only the *Relative* ; whereas
religion demands the *Absolute*. It is merely the
aggregate of the forces of Nature, or Matter ;
whereas Religion has for its object that which lies
behind Nature. Indeed, no more significant symptom of the inherent weakness of Mr. Spencer's
philosophy can be adduced than his assertion that,
from the Persistence of Force, the flowing meta
morphoses of Nature must follow as its corollary ;
that from the Absolute, the Relative could be de
duced. Who will presume to span the gulf that
separates the Relative from the Absolute ? That
Mr. Spencer should attempt to stretch a bridge
between the Creator and created, and assure you
that you may walk across in safety ; that he should

pretend to have linked the known with the un-known, or to have shown how Being passes into Appearance, must be, to reflective minds, sufficient evidence of those subtle fallacies, which analysis has disclosed at the root of his philosophy.

And now, having stripped Mr. Spencer's theory of the contradictions which have obscured it, it becomes necessary to ask what is its real nature? We have found that the Law of Evolution, to which, according to his theory, all the changes in the Universe conform, is really deducible from a *fixed* quantity of force under the form of coexistent forces of *attraction* and *repulsion, i.e.,* from a fixed quantity of Matter. We have found that the Persistence of Force is merely the sum total of the forces of Nature, and being Relative cannot be the object on which religion dwells. We have found, too, that as the causes of all changes lie in the antecedents of these changes, there can be no room for a First Cause at all. In other words, Mr. Spencer's theory is, that the Universe consists of a *fixed* quantity of Matter, which has existed *from all eternity*, which is *indestructible*, and which, through the antagonistic forces that compose it, *itself necessitates* the changes passed through and still going on. This is the old atheistic theory which has been more or less prevalent since the days of Epicurus. It is simply that of self-existent Matter, and is open to Mr. Spencer's own criticism that it is impossible to think or conceive a self-existent Universe, or Universe without a beginning.

Having shown the nature of Mr. Spencer's theory, we will now consider its validity. We have to determine whether a *fixed* quantity of Force, under the form of coexistent forces of *attraction* and *repulsion*, does, by the strict mechanical necessity which these forces are under of following the line of least resistance, thereby necessitate the variety, harmony, and beauty of the Universe or not. If it does, there is no room for a First Cause at all. If it does not, it remains with us to show where the mechanical theory is incompetent, and to point out why a First Cause is a necessity of thought. Belief in a First Cause can no longer rest on the old foundations of authority or tradition. We must give a reason for our faith or consent to resign it. And it is with this alternative in my mind, that I shall, in the few remaining pages of this essay, venture to lay before the reader some considerations that have strengthened my conviction that underneath the visible phenomena of the World lies the Divine Cause.

But before entering on this part of my subject it is important that I should notice certain errors in philosophizing which run through nearly all metaphysical and theological controversies, and to which a large part of the confusion at present existing in these matters, is due.

To commence with :—There are certain contradictions supposed to be inherent in the human understanding, and which have been adduced to
exemplify its limitations. Such are : that we cannot conceive Space without end, or an end to Space ;
that we can neither conceive Matter to be infinitely
divisible, nor yet can we conceive a particle so small
as not to admit of further division. Now, there is
no reason why these contradictions should exist,
nor does Nature anywhere else support such an
anomaly. It seems probable, therefore, that these
contradictions have arisen from some error in the
process of philosophizing, which has escaped notice.
At all events, a good deal may be urged for the
belief that one of these contradictions is true, little
as we may be able to imagine it. It is to be
observed, in the first place, that the senses (the
avenues through which knowledge of the external world comes to us) are strictly limited to the
environment. They are adapted to the finite, and
can give us knowledge of the finite only. It is
unphilosophical to give them an extension beyond
their original sphere. The eye, the ear, taste, and
touch, are each adapted to furnish information of a
special kind, and no other. It is true that in looking at solid objects we imagine we see the solidity,
which we only infer. This is merely because two
different senses have consolidated their separate
impressions ; and is quite legitimate. Our muscu-

lar sensations, from which we get the idea of Mat
ter by the resistance it offers, and consequently of
Space, when the resistance is absent, are strictly
limited to the environment, to the finite. It is.
unphilosophical, then, to assume that space is unlimited. The supposition has arisen, doubtless,.
from the fact that we have no knowledge of its.
definite limits. On the earth no line can be drawn
beyond which it is not, nor in the heavens can we
fix the boundary. And as it occupies an immensity
beyond the reach of the senses, stretching away
into regions where the telescope cannot follow it,
there has grown up the conception that it is without end. 'What we can see, yet cannot see over,
is as good as Infinite.' But we have *positive*
grounds for believing that it is finite. I am deeply
indebted to Mr. Spencer for having first pointed out
that a fixed quantity of Force in the Universe is a
datum of consciousness, and is *assumed* in every
step we take, either in action or speculation. All
proof that facts correspond to ideas, takes for
granted a fixed quantity of Force ; for, as he has
shown, if gravitation were to vary from moment to
moment, we should be certain of nothing. Every
inference would be vitiated, and all verification
would be impossible. The limitations of Force are
the limitations of the Matter and Motion ; and the
limitations of the Matter and Motion are the limitations of Space. For Space is only coextensive with

Matter, physicists being obliged to fill the interspaces between planet and star with an ethereal
medium, which is Matter in a very attenuated form.
Matter and Space being finite, there is no reason
for supposing the First Cause to be Infinite. It
is enough for us—poor, wandering light-gleams cast
up on this latest wave of time—to be permitted
to behold, and for a moment to enjoy, this in-
comparable panorama of Nature, and, lifting our
eyes above, to know it has a commensurate Cause
and humbly worship there ; but to affirm its infinitude, in the strict sense of that term, is to intro-
duce into philosophy, contradiction ; into theology,
the seeds of atheism.

Akin to this importation into Philosophy, (by
the imagination,) of the Infinite, is the projection of
the *Relative* into the domain of the *Absolute.*
Consider, for instance, what is called the relation of
Cause and Effect. This relation merely expresses
the *order* existing among the antecedents or con-
sequents of any natural circumstance or event.
It is a purely *Relative* relation, if I may use the
term, limited entirely to changes in the environment, but has been pushed illegitimately into the
plane of the Absolute ; and shallow sceptics indulge their subtlety by asking you what is the
cause of the First Cause ? This is unphilosophical,
and has arisen, no doubt, from the habit of tracing
back cause to cause among natural phenomena ;

quite legitimate in its own sphere, but which cannot be carried across the gulf that divides the
Relative from the Absolute. For by no tracing
back of antecedent to antecedent, were it to eternity, could you arrive at the Absolute, which arises
from the *intuition of cause* in the mind—a different
matter from any mere antecedents. It is the one
Real Cause, and is the Unity to which all things
are referred.

Another error that is prevalent in philosophical
and theological writings, is the lifting a question
aloof from its natural basis, and discussing it apart
from its natural relations. Why, for instance, insist on knowing whether Matter is *infinitely* divisible or not, when it is known to us as *finitely*
divisible; or *absolutely* solid, when it is known as
relatively solid? Why ask whether Space and
Time are entities, nonentities, or attributes; and
laboriously endeavour to prove that they can be
neither, when there is no reason that they should
be either? We know perfectly well what the
terms represent to us. We know what is meant by
a mathematical line, do we not, although length
without breadth is impossible?[1] Again, why divorce the Absolute from its necessary connexion
with the Relative, and treat it as a separate exist-

[1] Why deny, as some do, the existence of Mind, because it is
not an 'entity,' *i.e.* because it is not Matter?

ence, as Mansel has done in the following extract, which Mr. Spencer endorses?—

But these three conceptions, the Cause, the Absolute, the Infinite, all equally indispensable, do they not imply contradictions to each other when viewed in conjunction as attributes of one and the same Being? A cause cannot as such be Absolute, the Absolute cannot as such be a Cause. The Cause as such exists only in relation to its effect; on the other hand the conception of the Absolute implies a possible existence out of all relation. We attempt to escape from the apparent contradiction by introducing the idea of succession in Time. The Absolute exists first by itself, and afterwards becomes a cause. But here we are checked by the third conception, that of the Infinite. How can the Infinite become that which it was not from the first? If causation is a possible mode of being, that which exists without causing is not Infinite, that which becomes a cause has passed beyond its former limits, &c. &c.

Now, why should 'the Cause exist only in relation to its effect,' and yet the Absolute 'be a possible existence out of all relation'? Am not I, who think of the Absolute, related to it? Without the Relative there could be no Absolute. The existence of one involves that of the other. The first contradiction, in the extract just quoted, would not exist were the word Absolute used in its ordinary sense. An absolute monarch is one who is independent of his subjects, not one out of all relation to them. When applied to the First Cause, it merely means that he is independent of us, and that in Him 'we live, move, and have our being.' The second contradiction would be avoided if, instead of using the term Infinite, we used the phrase, 'of no known limits,' for the reasons which I have given above. The like criticism may be made on the following extract from the same author. He says :

How can Infinite Power be able to do all things and yet Infinite Goodness be unable to do evil? How can Infinite Justice exact the utmost penalty for every sin and yet Infinite Mercy pardon the sinner? How can Infinite Wisdom know all that is to come, and yet Infinite Freedom be at liberty to do or forbear? How is the existence of Evil compatible with that of an Infinitely perfect Being, for if he wills it he is not infinitely good, and if he wills it not, his will is thwarted and his sphere of action limited.

This is one of the old stock-arguments of the atheists, brought down on us by the use of the word Infinite. As I have shown, its use cannot be justified, and if we cut it out, the contradictions fall away of themselves. Besides, it is always unphilosophical to weave fantastic attributes for the First Cause, and then to try and press the facts of Nature into harmony with them. It is enough—is it not?—that our conception of the Divine Cause should be commensurate with the grandeur and glory of the Universe.

And now to return to the theory under consideration, viz., that it is a mechanical necessity, that a fixed quantity of Force, made up of antagonistic forces of attraction and repulsion, should pass through successive stages and transformations, and produce the beauty and harmony of the universe of Mind and Matter, without the necessity for a Divine Cause. In endeavouring to show the inadequacy of this theory, I shall limit myself to the arguments that are adapted to meet this particular form of Atheism. I know that the World may be viewed from many standpoints, and that, however viewed, it will show beautiful colours. Turned before the inward eye, Nature shows like a diamond, whose glowing facets chase one another with emulous lustre. We need not lack faith, for, like a loaded die, she will always turn up a Divine face. She is so alive with Deity that, sink a shaft where we will, we may draw the living waters from that spring, whose source is hidden. She has innumerable sides, is as good as she is beautiful, and beau tiful as she is wise. No system of thought can formulate her. All things refer to each, and each to all—a seamless web with no loose ends. At best she can but be poorly transcribed, never understood. She has upheld and still upholds uncounted theories, and all our philosophies are but beggars of her bounty.

A wider induction often reverses the first impressions of the senses and the intellect. The earth appears stationary, and the sun to revolve. Seen from a boat, the shore seems to be moving. Colour, to all appearance, is a property of bodies. These are illusions of the senses. There are also illusions of the intellect. Among these the most important is the belief that Mind is the *product* of Matter. This has been a commonplace of scientific materialists, since we have observed the intimate, even exact, correspondence between mental manifestations and physical states. We have discovered that the brain is the organ of the mind ; that if its nervous substance is pressed upon, the manifestations of mind and sensibility cease ; that if the pressure is removed the manifestations return. We have discovered that variations in the physical conditions are accompanied by corresponding variations in the mental ; and that in proportion to the size and complexity of the nervous centres is the strength and complexity of the mental power. Now, this correspondence between Matter and Mind fulfils the conditions of a scientific *cause.* Any variation in the physical antecedents is followed by a corresponding variation in the mental manifestations. This uniformity, like all other uniformities, is called a Law of Nature. Hence it has been assumed that, if we can account for the material World, we have thereby accounted for the phenomena of Mind. Mr. Spencer's theory of Evolution everywhere proceeds on this assumption. Now, plausible as this may appear, farther consideration will, I think, show that, instead of Matter being the *cause* of Mind, Mind is really the *cause* of Matter. For the problem is to account not only for the physical world, but for *me*—the thinking, sentient being who contemplates it.

On looking at the appearances of the World, we see them so, because our senses are constituted so. Were our senses different, the appearances of the world would be different. Were the eye differently constructed, colours would be different. Were it as large as the lens of a telescope, the moon were here, and near objects would be invisible. Were it like the lens of a microscope, common objects could not be surveyed at once, and the atmosphere would be opaque with germs. Were we devoid of muscular or tactual sensation, the world would be a beautiful fairy vision. Were we devoid of all our senses, it would be only a dream. We get hints of the same truth, in other ways. Time appears shorter to the old than to the young. In certain nervous derangements, the body seems to cover an acre of ground. De Quincey said that, when under the influence of opium, ' Space swelled, and was amplified to an extent of unutterable infinitude,' and an hour seemed protracted to an eternity.

As our senses make the *material* world for us ; so our sentiments and emotions make our *social*

and *moral* world. It is difficult to give an adequate
statement of this truth, on account of its complicated nature, and at present I shall limit myself to
merely indicating the direction in which it is to be
looked for. We get hints of it, in the influence of
abnormal states of mind on our relations with the
world. The benignant, cheerful face which life
presents to the sanguine, shows sinister and gloomy
to the man of bilious temperament. Wine rounds
off the stubborn angularity of the real world, and
flushes it *couleur de rose.* Under the influence of
insanity, slaves have imagined themselves emperors,
and were this affliction more common, it would be
at once seen, how entirely we ourselves create the
world we enjoy or bemoan. These hints are repeated and enforced in our daily experience. It is
notorious that the lover decks the brow of his
mistress with the flowers of his own fancy. The
divinity is not so much in the church or the creed
as in the possibilities of the soul. Our ideals, too,
are but the scintillations of our imagination, taking
their form and colouring from our temperament,
associations, sympathies, and education. We feel
painfully this truth when we remember the ideals
we have outgrown, and have seen one by one
departing. Who can conjure us back the generous
enthusiasm of boyhood, when men and things gave
off beautiful, prismatic radiations, and were not
yet seen in the white light of a more prosaic time ?

Why have these early delights lost their fascination ? The attributes that first attracted us, as far as we can tell, remain the same, but we alas! have changed. The beautiful, iridescent, soap-bubbles that we blew, have long since burst, and yet we have but transferred to new objects the old accustomed dreams. On the other hand, great ideas walk before us embodied, yet remain invisible, awaiting a happier time. The perception of the truth that we make our own ideals, is the first step in the emancipation of the mind from the thraldom of individuals, for we are apt ever after to distrust our idols.

As the constitution of the senses makes the *material* world, and the constitution of the sentiments, the *social* and *moral* world ; so, the constitution of the intellect makes the *Laws of Nature*, and, among them, the particular law under consideration, viz. the dependence of mental manifestations on physical states. According to the Evolution-hypothesis, all the Laws of Nature are *corollaries* of the great Law of Evolution. They are minor uniformities included in that all-embracing uniformity. The Law of Evolution, itself, is a corollary from a *fixed* quantity of force which is made up of antagonistic forces of *attraction* and *repulsion*. Now, if we can show that these two facts—the *fixed* quantity of force, and the *antagonistic* forms—depend for their existence on the

constitution of our minds, it will necessarily follow
that all the Laws of Nature, and, among them,
this particular law of the dependence of mental
manifestations on physical states, depend on the
constitution of our minds. That they do so depend,
may be drawn from Mr. Spencer's own admissions.
He says (§ 74):

probably the conception of antagonistic forces is originally derived from the antagonism of our flexor and ex-
tensor muscles,—

i.e. from muscular sensation—the lowest form of
mind. How purely it results from the constitution of
our minds, appears from the fact that, otherwise, it is
altogether inconceivable. Mr. Spencer says (§ 74)·

We cannot truly represent one ultimate unit of matter
as drawing another while resisting it. Nevertheless this
belief is one we are compelled to entertain.

The Law of Evolution may be a corollary from
a fixed quantity of force in antagonistic forms,
but the antagonistic forms themselves can be a
corollary from nothing. For there is no reason
why force should be presented to us under these
forms, except that we are constituted to see it *so.*

The fact again that the quantity of Force in
the Universe is *fixed,* depends absolutely on the
constitution of the mind. As Mr. Spencer has
shown, it is a *datum* of consciousness which cannot
be *proved* at all. It is assumed in every argument,

every proof, and every inference. It is a pure
intuition of the mind. Thus we see that the
appearances of the material world, the forms of the
social and moral world, and the very Laws of
Nature themselves, all depend upon the constitution of our minds. Mind asserts herself, and trails
Matter and the Laws of Matter captive at her heels.
And therefore the problem of the world reduces
itself, not to an explanation of material things, but
to an explanation of the Human Mind itself. It may
be urged that, as the constitution of the human
mind is fixed by the same *necessity* which determines the evolution of matter, it is therefore unphilosophical to raise the question as to what the
world would be, were we differently constituted.
I admit, of course, that if the Law of Evolution
were true, it would necessarily follow that the
nervous structures, like all other forms of matter,
would follow the laws of force in general. But I
deny that the being, the thinking, sentient existence,
—which is the other side of these forces—would
follow. And this is precisely the point at issue.
Does it *necessarily* follow from a fixed quantity of
force made up of antagonistic forces, that, at a
certain point in the physical transformations of the
Universe, what is known as a molecular motion
will give rise to a ' shock in consciousness ?' Does
it *necessarily* follow that when ' the integration of
matter and concomitant dissipation of motion '

have reached a certain stage of complexity, the
feeling of pleasure, or of self-preservation, or of
pride, or of hate, shall arise? And might not the
same physical conditions be accompanied by different mental attributes altogether, as far as the
Law of Evolution is concerned? Is it a *necessary*
deduction from the Law of Evolution, that the
next further development in the brain of an ape
shall give rise to the new feelings of respect, honour,
reverence, beauty, conscientiousness? Is there any
necessary reason in the theory of Evolution why
the appetites and passions should be ranked as *low*
feelings, and the sentiments and finer feelings as
high ones? There is and can be no possible
relationship whatever between the character of the
molecular motion, and the character of the *feelings*
answering to it. In fact, the human mind cannot
be accounted for at all. Only the Maker of man
can at all understand it. The materialists, however, nothing daunted, have attempted to explain
the feelings of the mind, as well as the transformations of matter. I shall take Mr. Spencer's account
of them. It will be seen that he reduces the more
complex of them to modes of *pleasure* and *pain*,
differently represented. Thus, the love of property
consists of representations of the different kinds of
pleasure to be derived from its possession. Courage
arises out of the *pleasure* we derive from the sympathy and approbation of others. Fear springs

from representations of *pain* to be suffered. Pride is evolved from the *gratifications* that attend continual successes ; humility from the *pain* attending perpetual failures. The religious sentiment is prompted largely by representations of divine approval, joined with the *happiness* to be secured by that approval. Justice 'consists of representations of those emotions which others feel, when actually or prospectively allowed or forbidden the activities by which pleasure is to be gained, or pain escaped.' Having derived the feelings of the mind from modes of pleasure and pain, we now expect Mr. Spencer to show us how Pleasure and Pain are *necessitated* by the Law of Evolution. He has nowhere made the attempt. We naturally ask, why we should have these feelings ? No answer is returned, but we are put off with a mere generalisation of the *conditions* that call them into exercise. In his chapter on ' Pleasures and Pains,' in the first volume of his ' Principles of Psychology,' he says, ' generally speaking, pleasures are the *concomitants* of medium activities,' and concludes, that they guide an animal to its benefit, while, on the other hand, pains attend actions injurious to the animal. This as little explains the feelings of pleasure and pain themselves, as the conditions of a good appetite explain the feeling of hunger, or the attractions of personal appearance or character explain the feeling of love. The human mind being an inexplicable mystery, the *facts* of the mind remain for our consideration ; and from these facts, all that we can know of ourselves, and our relation to the Universe, must be deduced. This knowledge, which lies quite beyond the domain of Science, may be reduced to three heads. First, Final Cause, and the hierarchy of means and ends ; secondly, true *causes*, as distinguished from scientific *occasions* ; and lastly, the existence and attributes of a Supreme Cause.

Science, as we have seen above, has no room for a First Cause. She must, therefore, necessarily reject all belief in Final Cause. Nothing seems to annoy Mr. Spencer more than what he calls a ' teleological interpretation.' To say that the eye exists for sight, the ear for hearing, or the legs for locomotion, is to incur his undisguised contempt. He has arrived at the belief that these things result from the ' survival of the fittest,' and have been embodied in the race by hereditary transmission—as happy adaptations, behind which there is no Mind. Now, although everything in Nature subserves not one, but many purposes, still a light general survey of the whole discloses certain broad intentions—a hierarchy of means and ends, each end being, in its turn, only a means to a higher. Thus, minerals exist for the support of vegetables ; vegetables for the support of animals ; and all for the use, delight, and instruction of man. Hunger and thirst, the lower appetites, envy, fear, pride, aggressiveness, are *means* to self-preservation and the continuance of life ; the continuance of life, to ascension of mind and increase of understanding ; increase of understanding, to perception of moral law ; perception of moral law, to spirituality and religion.

But besides final causes (which require some experience to handle, and which must be pressed very gently to get their fragrance), the facts of the mind furnish us with the real *causes* of things, as distinguished from scientific *occasions*. Mr. Spencer somewhere describes the results which follow the fact that one member of a homogeneous tribe displays an unusual facility for the making of weapons. This simple circumstance is represented by him as the *cause* of the division of labour which follows throughout the whole tribe. It is in reality only the *occasion* ; the *cause* being the inherent capability in each individual of becoming a specialised worker—being, in short, the power and adaptability of the mind. We must look to the facts of the mind, and not to scientific principles, for the causes of human action. How are we to explain eating, but from hunger ; fear, but from love of life ; contempt of danger, but from elevation of mind ; excitement, but from sympathy ; prayer, but from religion.

And, lastly, the facts of the mind are the final

appeal on the question we are considering, viz.,
the existence and attributes of a Supreme Cause.
Of course, the existence of a Supreme Cause, like
the existence of mind in our fellow-man, is purely
a matter of inference. It cannot be seen, or in
any way be made apparent to the senses. It cannot be reached by Science, which deals entirely
with these same sense-impressions. It cannot be
deduced primarily from the world around us, for,
as I have shown, the world follows the mind like a
shadow, or reflects it like a mirror. If inferred at
all, it must be from the constitution of the mind.
Let us consider it. The mind .is made up of an
intuition of Causation, and a scale of Sensations,
running from the lowest muscular and tactual sensations up through the special senses, appetites,
and passions, to the highest and finest feelings and
sentiments. The intuition of Causation demands
a Supreme Cause for the impressions and sensations we derive from the Universe around us. This
inference cannot be escaped without the dissolution
of our intelligence itself. Belief in a Supreme
Cause falls as easily and naturally on the open
human mind as sleep.. It is the last result of
philosophy to bring us round to faith in the simple
intuitions of the mind. After wandering through
startling, highly-coloured systems, whose novelty
and ingenuity amuse and detain us for an hour,
we come home to this at last. The weight to be

attached to this simple intuition, in its bearings on the question of a Supreme Cause, is significantly illustrated by the attitude Mr. Spencer has taken in regard to it. His scientific method excludes all conception of a First Cause. It rejects also the intuitions as a philosophical instrument, professing to interpret all phenomena in terms of Matter, Motion, and Force. And yet he feels bound to assert a Supreme Cause for the impressions left on our senses by the visible Universe. This he can do only by breaking through his own method, and taking down, from the higher region of the mind, the intuition of Causation, and using it as a philosophical instrument. Indeed, he goes so far as to say that it is one of the postulates which must be assumed before Philosophy can commence, and without which it is impossible.

As the intuition of Causation demands a Supreme Cause, so the scale of Sensations demands that the *attributes* of this Cause shall be commensurate with the dignity of the human mind. The materialists, who believe that we are products of the great impersonal laws which ply their everlasting labours on all sides of us, object to our investing the Supreme Being with human attributes. They say it is a degrading of the Creator to the level of the creature. Those of them who, like Mr. Spencer, are unable to escape the belief in a Supreme Cause, still prefer to consider that Cause

as an Unknown Force, without attributes, or with
attributes of which we can have no conception.
My reply to this objection lies in the proof I have
given above, that these impersonal Laws of Nature
follow the mind, exist through the mind, and are
what they are, by the mind.   The materialists put
the cart before the horse.   The Laws of Nature do
not create the mind of Man, but the mind of Man is
created to perceive, among other things, the Laws of
Nature.   We must first recognise the God, whose
throne is upheld by the pillars of Justice, Goodness,
and Truth, and then we can with equal reverence recognise His instruments on earth—the 'impersonal'
Laws of Nature.   It may be said that to endow the
Deity with attributes commensurate with the human
mind, is to endow Him with human appetites and
passions.   A little consideration will show that this
is not necessarily the case.   There is in Nature
and the Human Mind a *Public Element* which
works for universal, and not particular, ends.   It is
quite distinct from the lower attributes, which
minister to the selfish interests of the individuals.
It has different aspects.   One of these is Beauty,
which is present everywhere, and is an expression
of the Soul that is at the centre of things.   But
there are other sides.   A glance over the animal
and vegetable world reveals the existence of a
Power which works for the general good.   This is
seen in the proportion which is everywhere kept

between animal and vegetable life, thus preserving the proper composition of the atmosphere. It is seen in the proportion kept among the different races of animals, by the balance between the powers of aggression and defence. In Man, the appetites and passions which minister to his *private* ends, are balanced by the unselfish sentiments of Justice, Goodness, and Truth, which minister to the *general* welfare. The existence of a spirit working everywhere for Beauty, Love, Justice, and Truth, gives us the hint of the attributes of the Supreme Cause.

CONSIDERATIONS ON THE CONSTITU TION OF THE WORLD.

I WISH, in this essay, to offer some considerations on the constitution of the World. But before doing so, I should like to clear the way by briefly pointing out what I believe to be the leading misconceptions of those thinkers who have attempted a theory of the Universe on scientific principles. I feel this to be necessary for several reasons. The leaders of this school are men of high intellectual endowments. They are active propagandists, and are all acknowledged masters in their own departments. They are welded into one compact power by the general agreement of their principles, and have at present more followers, perhaps, than any other school of thought. Personally, I am very much interested in every scientific discovery. I believe we owe our material prosperity as much to the labours of the scientist, as to the efforts of the legislator, and the application of scientific principles to the arts, promises to be as fruitful of benefit in the future, as it has been in the past. Besides, I am myself engaged in a profession, which is a constant training in the appreciation of scientific facts and in the weighing of scientific evidence, and which is most deeply indebted to scientific research. My only objection is to the application of scientific methods of thought to the solution of the Problem of Life. I shall therefore confine myself exclusively to the mode of interpretation that lies at the root of all scientific philosophy.

Perhaps, for my present purposes, I may be allowed to divide the human mind, roughly, into Outer Senses, Inner Senses, and the Understanding. The Outer Senses are those of touch, taste, sight, smell, and hearing ; the Inner Senses are the higher feelings of the mind—Beauty, Love, Reverence, Duty, Sublimity, and the like ; the Understanding is the faculty that arranges the material supplied by or through these respective media. Now, scientific thinkers interpret the phenomena of the World from the Outer Senses alone. This is their first fundamental error. In the scale of creation, Man is the highest ; and in Man, the Inner Senses. Many of the lower animals have as acute Outer Senses as man, and the higher among them have a considerable amount of Understanding. But, just as before the Outer Senses were developed (and many sentient creatures are wanting in these, having only the lowest form of tactual sensation), there could be no perception of form, colour, &c. ; so, until the higher Inner Senses are developed,

there can be no apprehension of the higher qualities
of Nature. It is clearly, then, as absurd to interpret
from the outer senses, which are a mid-point in the
scale of mind, as it would be to interpret from the
point of view of a monkey, which is a mid-point in
the scale of intelligent creatures. I conclude, therefore, that the highest and deepest knowledge possible for us, will be that furnished by the highest
faculties of the highest human intelligence. I have
said that scientific thinkers base their interpretation
on the material furnished through the Outer Senses
alone. For instance, what is the Law of Gravitation,
but a deduction drawn from the *observation* that all
bodies tend to approximate ? The law that ' force
follows the line of least resistance,' too, what is it
but a deduction drawn from the *observation* of the
constant action of bodies on one another ? Again,
are not all the laws of physics—heat, chemistry,
electricity— and of botany, physiology, &c., founded
on data furnished exclusively by the outer senses
of sight, taste, smell, or touch ? The microscope,
scalpel, and retort, what are they but aids to the
Outer Senses merely ?

The Evolution-hypothesis is the latest and most
complete attempt to account for the phenomena of
the Universe on Scientific inductions. It undertakes to account for both physical and mental
phenomena, by Physical Laws alone. Having
observed the constant connection between the

manifestations of mind and the physical conditions of the brain, and concluding that mental phenomena have a physical side, it assumes that, if it can account for the latter, it has explained the former. But the fallacy of this is apparent. For when I ask myself what is the *nature* of the force that causes bodies to approximate, I cannot tell, nor can I at all comprehend the *character* of the force that follows the line of least resistance. But the Spiritual forces within me, which are the other sides, so to speak, of these Physical forces, I directly *know*. So that the Evolution-hypothesis undertakes to account for what I know by what I do not know, which is clearly absurd. Doubtless, there is a difference between the physical side of what we know as a feeling of hate, and one of love ; between a feeling of disgust, and one of sublimity or beauty. Science may ultimately point out this difference, but no scalpel will ever show the difference in the *nature* of the feelings themselves—the fact that the one set is of a *low*, the other of a *high*, character. This difference in *ranking* is made known to us by the fixed Scale of Feelings in the mind, but could not possibly be discovered by any observations made by the Outer Senses. It is perceived entirely by the Inner Senses— a region of mind which scientific thinkers have stigmatised as mystical, which they have excluded as a philosophical instrument, but on which they are compelled to draw

at every step.   The attempt, then, to interpret the
phenomena of life from the outer senses, is the first
fundamental error in scientific and materialistic
philosophies.   I shall proceed now to the second.

All philosophy is founded on a belief in the
correspondence between the Mind and the World.
Unless the qualities of Nature had their correlatives
in the human mind, there could be no interpretation.
That this correspondence exists, is seen in the
power we can exert over the physical elements.
We can decompose, rearrange, and recombine them,
proving that the laws *within* us answer to those
without us.   It is seen in the control we can exercise over the lower animals ; in our power to charm
or tame them after the laws of their nature.   It is
seen in the *identical expression* of character throughout the whole animal kingdom.   We see among
men eagle faces, lion faces, fox faces, monkey faces,
and the character corresponds.   It is seen in Language and the use of metaphors.   It is seen in the
power we exert over our fellows, and the identity
of thought, sentiment, and impulse, on which we rely
in our appeals to them.   This correspondence
begins low down in our physical, and ascends to
the subtlest intuitions of our spiritual nature.   Ears
are found in air, eyes in light.   For every male
there is a female.   The Senses are adapted to forms,
colours, and sounds ; the Understanding, to the
order among the forces of Nature ; Beauty, to their

harmony and infinite variety. Compassion and Justice have their sphere in the welfare of our fellows ; Reverence, in our superiors ; and Worship, in God.

This correspondence of the Mind to the World is admitted by scientific thinkers, but their theory of it, though simple, is inadequate. They assert that the forces of the environment of any organism coming in contact with that organism, initiate changes in it ; that these changes are adapted to the changes among the forces of the environment ; and that in the higher organisms they constitute the Mind. Now, were the human mind simply an organised system of changes, their explanation might suffice. But it is more than this. And here is precisely the weak point in the Theory of Evolution. For this *power of adaptation* is not the whole, or even the most important part of the mind. There are, besides, the Intuitions and Feelings, of which the *power of adaptation* is merely the *instrument.* These intuitions and feelings are *fixed and unchanging*, are there by the will of God, and cannot be explained at all. Scientific thinkers assume them without attempting to account for them. They assume, for instance, the feeling of hunger in an animal, and then show you how its organisation is adapted to catch its prey. They assume the love of life prompting it to escape from its enemies, and then show you the adaptation by which this is effected. They assume the feelings of pleasure and pain, and then show you the conditions of the nervous system necessary to induce or maintain them. They assume the feelings of honour and shame, and then show you that the actions prompted by them differ according to the circumstances and necessities of tribes and nations. They assume the feeling of beauty, and then show you the conditions and associations under which it arises. They assume the existence of a fixed Scale in the mind ; rank selfishness and sensuality *low*—justice, love, beauty, and reverence *high* ; but give no reason for doing so. So that, from the lowest animal up to man, the feelings of hunger, love of life, fear, honour and shame, pleasure and pain, beauty, the Scale in the mind, &c., are *assumed*, but not *accounted for*, by the Evolution-hypothesis. This is the second fundamental weakness in the theory.

The correspondence between the Mind and the World, then, cannot be accounted for from the World. Our alternative is to account for the World from the Mind. But before proceeding further, I wish to show in detail that we can get an insight into the World only by looking at the *fixed intuitions* and *feelings* of the mind, and not at the outer *circumstances* which call them forth, and which are inconstant, contradictory, and dependent on situation and condition.

Opinions as to what is Right and Wrong have varied in every country, and in every age. The Spartans were encouraged to steal ; the Chinese, to deceive. Among the Tartars under Zenghis Khan, it was not considered wrong to break one's word or seize another's goods, to do a person an injury, or commit murder ; but it was a sin, and even a capital crime, to lean against a whip, to strike a horse with its bridle, or break one bone against another. Murder is considered an act of heroism among the Polynesians. Macaulay says that, among the Highlanders of the seventeenth century, robbery was held to be a calling, not only innocent, but honourable. In Formosa, it was believed that the debauchery of children was agreeable to the gods ; while there was a sort of hell for those who had dressed in calico and not in silk, who had presumed to look for oysters, or had undertaken any business without consulting the songs of birds. Among the ancient Massagetæ, as in the ideal republic of Plato, women were held in common ; and Plutarch relates that Cato lent his wife to Hortensius. In China, filial piety is the highest virtue ; while amongst the ancient inhabitants of India, the sick were killed, and those rendered infirm by age were sacrificed and eaten by their kinsmen.

The same truth is seen where the diversity of opinion as to the *morality* of actions has been the

result of National Interest. Socrates, when asked
how he could distinguish those things which were
wrong from those things which were right, could
not tell, but referred his interrogator to the decisions
of the laws of his country. At Rome, the un-
married were under legal penalties. In Persia, next
to personal courage, the highest honour was to have
a numerous offspring. De Tocqueville says, ' Envy
is the vice of democracies ; ' and consequently, in
America, pride is a disparagement to a man ;
whereas, in the old feudal countries of Europe, it is
almost a virtue. Among the barbarians, who overran Europe, and established themselves on the
ruins of the Roman Empire, the sole appeal in
every dispute was to physical force. Hence the
trials by combat, and the ordeals of hot iron and
boiling water. Right and wrong became a matter
of strength of arm or thickness of skin.

The same truth is exemplified by the way in
which Morality is affected by Religion. In ancient
Egypt, whoever killed an ibis or vulture was put
to death. The marriage of sisters was consecrated
in honour of Isis. The Assyrians and Persians
married their mothers ; the former out of respect
for Semiramis, the latter as deemed more honour
able by Zoroaster. The material characteristics of
a country affect religious beliefs. Montesquieu
says that metempsychosis is adapted to the climate
of the Indies, as they can breed few cattle there.

A religious law prevents their killing and eating their cattle, as the flesh is insipid, but the milk and butter nutritious. The soil of Athens was barren, and it was a religious maxim with the Athenians that those who offered small presents to the gods honoured them more, than those who sacrificed an ·ox. Montezuma insisted that his religion was best for Mexico, and that of the Spaniards for their own country.

Farther, the same truth appears, if, leaving special instances, we take a general survey of the religions of the world. The gods of the savages are the reflections of the ideas and circumstances of the tribe. They are usually brutal and revengeful, and the same means are taken to appease their wrath as that of offended chiefs. The physical and mental powers of the Greeks were personified in all their free and graceful harmony in their mythology. The rough sincerity of the Norsemen appears in every legend. As character and culture ascend, Religion alters. The Elohim of the Jews at first represented the powers of Nature. When these powers were afterwards seen to be *moral*, Jehovah supplanted Elohim, who was then transformed into something resembling our modern Devil.

We see, too, that the Social and Political institutions of nations (and therefore their notions of Morality and Honour) have been the fruit of their dominant Idea. The laws of Lycurgus were all framed for military supremacy. They necessitated poverty and temperance, trained the youth to endurance and cunning, to obedience and contempt of death. The Jewish laws all pointed to religion; the Chinese aimed at public tranquillity. The institutions of the barbarians were the expression of the idea they brought with them—personal liberty. Military service was voluntary and personal, while at Rome it was fixed and impersonal—to the State. Hence Tacitus seemed surprised that the chiefs of the German tribes should receive, from their companions-in-arms, services that would be rendered to the Roman Emperor only by freedmen or slaves.

The truth I am striving to illustrate (that we must look at the fixed *feelings* and *intuitions* of the mind, and not at the other *circumstances* in which they are clothed) is seen in the influence exerted over our opinions by *Custom.* The religion of pagan Rome, for example, whence its acceptance by the millions? Largely, the chance that a band of brigands happened to bring with them a handful of rites from Etruria; these pigments, thrown in at the fountain head, were carried down through the succeeding generations, tincturing the stream. Indeed, the preponderating element in all traditional masses of opinion, is Custom, and not Insight. This is seen in literature and art. Schools of music and art have their periods of regnancy and culmination, and for the time being are the standards of taste. In medicine, bleeding and calomel were the universal practice of physicians, for generations, but in our time they have almost completely gone out. We have almost deified Shakespeare, but our ancestors, consistently with their habits of thought, considered Addison and Pope his superiors.

Class distinctions and Social organizations modify our opinions. The influence of a powerful and all-reaching organization on opinion is nowhere better seen than in the doctrine of Papal Infallibility. We clothe the aristocracy with attributes and radiances, which are not found in the individuals composing it. The world has always attributed to rulers and statesmen greater intellect and refinement than can be strictly accorded to them. The same is true, too, of the clergy. Military men come to the front in time of war, and an idea gathers around them, which falls away in times of peace.

Having seen, then, that our opinions as to the *nature* of actions vary from age to age, according to Utility, Religion, Custom, Culture, &c., and leaving the natural compensations to be considered farther on, I wish here especially to insist, that this variety is only in the *form*, not in the *essence* ; in the *outer* Facts, not in the *inner* Tendencies ; in the beads, and not in the wires on which they are strung, which are everywhere and in all ages the same. The feeling of Worship is always the same,

whether its object be the fetish of the savage, the
sun among the Persians, the bull Apis of the Egyptians, or the Jehovah of the Jews. The feeling of
Right and Wrong is always the same, and conscience has the same reaction, whether it be for
leaning against a whip among the Tartars, killing
a cat among the Egyptians, picking up sticks on
the Sabbath among the Jews, or murder among ourselves. The feeling of Admiration is always the
same, whether it be for physical prowess, personal
beauty, practical wisdom, or intellectual refinement.
The feeling of Hope is always the same, whether
its object be the happy hunting-grounds of the Indians, the Valhalla of the Norsemen, where the
brave drink mead out of cups made from the skulls
of those they have killed in battle, or the paradise
of Mahomet, with its feasting and dark-eyed
houris. And so on, upwards and downwards,
throughout the whole gamut of intuitions and
feelings.

We are now in a position to get a clearer view
of the Constitution of the World, as we have only
to deal with the simple *intuitions* and *feelings*
of the mind, and not with the variety of *forms* in
which these elements clothe themselves from age
to age, and which we have seen to be uncertain,
contradictory, and dependent on circumstance and
condition.

The World is constituted of a series of Balances,

on an ascending scale, ranging from the lowest ground-plane of Physics up to the finest intuitions of the Human Mind. This is the secret mechanism that maintains harmony among the heavenly bodies and moral order among mankind. Life is so saturated with this principle, that it may be found in the finest particles. The health and harmony of the whole consist in the maintenance of this balance at every point. Any loss of poise would be chaos or insanity. Let me illustrate more in detail the universality of this principle.

Every sun, every planet, every satellite, is kept in its place by the antagonism of the centripetal and centrifugal motions ; and by the balance of these forces the universe is sustained. In physics the law that ' action and reaction are equal and opposite,' runs through every mass and atom. It is seen in the ebb and flow of the sea, the alternation of day and night, sleep and wake, systole and diastole of the heart, inspiration and expiration. Every cell of every vegetable and every animal has its period of motion and rest, action and inaction, supply and expenditure.

The nervous system is constructed on the same principle. Its simplest definite form consists of nerve centres or corpuscles, and nerve fibres ; the latter transmitting impressions, the former redistributing or absorbing them ; these two balance one another. This simple type of structure is repeated in the higher and highest organizations, forming in these a chain, in which the highest centre —the brain—is linked with and has organized relations with all below it. The whole is a balance, and every part. Organic life, too, is maintained by the balance of the forces supplied by the blood, and those expended in performing the vital functions. Mr. Spencer, looking at the mind abstractedly as made up of states of consciousness, justly says, 'All mental action whatever is definable as the continuous *differentiation* and *integration* of states of consciousness.' 'These are the two antagonistic processes by which consciousness subsists—the centrifugal and centripetal actions by which its balance is maintained. That there may be the material for thought, consciousness must every moment have its state differentiated. And for the new state hence resulting to become a thought, it must be integrated with before-experienced states. This perpetual alternation is the condition of all thought, from the very lowest to the very highest. It is distinctly typified in that oscillation between two states constituting the simplest conceivable form of consciousness, and it is illustrated in the most complex thinkings of the most cultivated men.'

If we look at the conditions necessary to health of mind, we shall see the same principle illustrated. The variety. of the world is endless and perplexing.

It would become unhealthy and oppressive, did we not gather up its details into masses, and, by resting on broad principles, relieve the nervous tension attendant on minute incessant observation. The child, the slave of its eyes and ears, without general ideas as a compensating rest, is soon exhausted and falls asleep. To go through a picture gallery is too great a strain on the uncultivated eye. The mind wanders up and down along the diversity of colour and form, and finds no rest. The result is a headache. But the critic bringing with him fixed principles of judgment, around which the details arrange themselves, disposes with ease of the embarrassing variety. The cultivated physician has no difficulty in charging his memory with the most complicated symptoms, and can carry the particulars of many cases without confusion. The novice, with native powers of memory equally strong, would find this almost impossible. The secret of imparting knowledge consists in nicely balancing the two poles of thought. Rules and exercises, principles and illustrations, general ideas and detailed facts, should be so rapidly alternated as to admit of no preponderance of either. Mental disease, too, shows the necessity of a balance. For what is insanity, but unceasing motion of mind without rest, or fixity without healthy change?

The agitation of states discloses the same fact. Political ideas (as in France at the time of the

Revolution) sometimes make men so frenzied with
excitement, that they surge up into huge unwieldy
masses, incapable of control. The excitement
caused by war is commonly attended with tempo
rary loss of head. The same effect attends reli
gious excitements and panics. But a reaction soon
sets in, and when the change of circumstances holds
the mirror up to these extravagances, their exag-
geration becomes apparent, and the swing in the
opposite direction restores the equilibrium. It
has been often said that an age of political licence
is generally followed by a despotism. In all this,
we see that mere size is of no account. The law
holds good for masses, because each atom is poised.

If we look at the processes of Science, we shall
see the same principle illustrated. On the circumference of things is an infinite variety of forms.
Men of science starting from different points, and
removing the outermost stratum of details, find it
resting on, and springing from, a more uniform
structure. The diversity of animal and vegetable
forms are found to spring from a few species ; the
variety of physical forms, from a few forces ; and
of chemical compounds, from a few elements.
Penetrating farther and farther, they come to a belt
where the deeper laws of each science merge into
and overlap one another. On piercing this, the
centre is reached, a unity of force, of which all the
superincumbent forms are manifestations. At each

point of the process, particulars rest on and are balanced by generalizations, and generalizations. at last rest on Unity.

Society is led and dazzled by Imagination ; but the antidote is proximity and insight. We go in flocks to this or that shrine, but once behind the veil, we see the illusion, and cannot again be tempted. At Rome, the scarlet indulgences of the Papacy were witnessed by the pilgrims who were constantly passing and repassing. By stripping off the halo that surrounded the pontiff, this hastened the Reformation. Every sect has its hero, every household its idolatry. Freshness of association, by breaking up these groups and letting in the light, reveals the blemishes and limitations.

Ascending still higher to the sphere of the Intuitions, we find the same polarity. The feelings of the mind split themselves into two antithetical halves, the action and interaction of which constitute our higher life. The one set minister to our *private* interests and personal welfare ; the other to *public* interests and the welfare of the whole. The one set are *material*, and part of organisation ; the other *spiritual*, and part of God The World is constituted so that each separate being shall maintain its own individuality, and at the same time be subservient to the harmony of the whole. Our personality, being of such prime importance, has a whole battalion of feelings, jealously guarding it—Selfishness, Love of Life, Combativeness, Pride, Envy, Vanity, and Fear. These are not spiritual ; but are merely the mental *instruments* of self-preservation.   They are known through the mind, but are not properly parts of it. But their union and natural strength tending to give them a preponderance, a balance was needed. It is provided in the spiritual part of our nature,— the instrument of God by which the harmony of His moral creation is sustained.   It has different sides, and takes different forms—Religion, Justice, Conscience, Honour, Compassion, Shame.   These antagonize and balance private inclination or interest, point to point.   In the world, the failings and errors of our fellows are met by our Compassion ; their helplessness and oppression, by Love and Pity.   In ourselves, any temptation to breaches of decorum is counteracted by Shame ; to infraction of the arbitrary laws which every organized society establishes for the welfare of the whole, by Honour ; to violation of the deep relations of man to man, by Conscience and Justice ; to contempt of the laws of God, by Religion.   Speaking of these feelings as a whole, we may call them the *Moral Sentiment.*   In itself, it is quite unaccountable and independent of circumstances, but, as I have shown above, clothes itself from the wardrobe of utility, religion, custom, &c.   The plastic power of this sentiment secures progress by adapting itself to the new wants of new ages and conditions. It follows insight and belief, which it translates into action. All moral and religious codes have been better or worse transcripts of the beliefs held as to the nature of the Universe at the time of their promulgation. To follow in action the laws of the Uni verse,—that is Morality. This sentiment is superior to the individual, as the Creator is superior to the thing created. If I do what I believe to be a wrong, I become less—less in manhood, less in influence, and less in power. If I choose the right and generous deed, in spite of personal inconveni- ence, I feel a throb and enlargement of heart and will. If I take my stand on a truth, I partake of its power, have the Universe under my feet as support, and am superior to Fate. It is this senti- ment in us that checks ambition, when it becomes leagued with unworthy means, restrains the im- periousness of the passions, and counteracts the centralising tendencies of selfishness. It is seen in men's devotion to a principle at the expense of their personal happiness; in the power of love, and the sacrifices it prompts. Its preponderance in history has given the world its heroes. In pro- portion to men's earnestness and depth of thought, have they risen above personal and selfish con- siderations, and Politics, Religion, Art, Science, Philosophy, and Philanthropy, have all had their martyrs.

Again the same balance is seen in Action. Every natural power is evil, until the law of its appearance, action, and conditions—in short, until its *cause* is known.   Steam is dangerous, but know its law, and its unregulated power may be converted into an instrument of good.   The lightning-rod conducts the obnoxious fluid harmlessly to the ground, and, diluted by art, its healthy currents are made to circulate through the body.   On board our ships, we mock the threatening waves, and carry fire in our safety lamps through the midst of explosive gases.   And, indeed, all the arts (which are merely applied science) shield us from the sharp edges of the elements which they balance and antagonise.

Looking over periods of time, observe, too, how the present is the balance and equivalent of the whole past, as the stamped coin is of the mountains of ore from which it was extracted.   The good of the present is the expressed result of all that has gone before.   Liturgies are the picked prayers of the ages, language the picked words, law the picked processes, machinery the picked methods, and government the picked policies.

In the masses that constitute society, the same law is seen in the balance of Custom and Innovation.   We love novelty, but hate change.   Society is a horde of theorists, each of whom is rabid with his scheme of social, moral, or political regeneration,

but in which each has an antidote against the con
tagious madness of his neighbour in Custom,—or
the holding fast to the old. Society is a tree that
puts forth its new cells, leaves, and buds, only as
fast as the old have attained sufficient rigidity for
their support. This balance of the old and new is
seen in every cell, in every fibre, in every leaf, in
every organ of every animal and vegetable. It
makes its appearance in politics in the parties of
Conservatism and Reform,—in those who stand on
the old and those who embrace the new. It has
become a political axiom that orderly progress is
best secured by the healthy play and interaction of
these two principles, which are not capricious or
accidental, but have their roots in fundamental
tendencies of the human mind.

As the *Moral Sentiment* is the balance power
in the Mind, so *Might* is the balance power in the
World. We have many enemies. Besides the
passions and unregulated desires within us, there is
the obstinacy of natural powers and the pressure of
aggressive enemies without us. The power, be it
physical, moral, or intellectual, that can most effect-
ually counterbalance these, we call Might ; and in
action, it is the practical measure of Right. The
animal that can give most protection to the herd,
becomes the leader, and has the right to dominate.
Among savages, the chief being best able to promote the interests of the tribe, and protect it from

surrounding enemies, has the right to impose his
will on the rest. Among civilised nations the same
thing holds. The English colonists have won their
right to rule wherever they have appeared, by
being the greatest power to organise and ameli-
orate. The Romans, fallen into luxury and effemi-
nacy, with every social tie relaxed, and the nation
ready to fall to pieces from internal decay, yielded
the right to rule to the rude but genuine valour of
the barbarians who overran the empire. The Turk,
having lost his Might, has lost his Right to rule in
Europe. The relation between *Mights* and *Rights*
is interesting, but as it is not immediately connected with my present purpose, I shall throw my
thoughts on it into a very small compass. Firstly,
I find that Political-morality lags behind Constitutional-morality ; and Constitutional-morality, behind Social-morality. Nations appeal to arms,
classes to constitutional weapons, and citizens to
laws. The first is an appeal to Force, the second
to Self-interest, the last to Reason. The morality
of the first sanctions diplomacy or finesse ; of the
second, selfishness ; and of the last, social distinction.
What would be dishonourable in the citizen, would
be prudent in the partisan, and almost a virtue in
the diplomatist. Secondly, nations, classes, and
individuals appeal to Force in proportion to the
disparity of their Mights ; to arbitration, or Law,
in proportion to their equality. The history of

nations is a long commentary on this text. The principle, however, is modifiable by civilisation, which increases the tendency to appeal to arbitration. In the constitutional changes of this country, there was no appeal to Reason until the relative Mights were settled. In the struggles for Magna Charta, power of the Commons, Catholic emancipation, Reform Bill, Free Trade, the appeal was to open force, or to the sword, thinly disguised under constitutional forms. At the present, any infraction of these rights is quietly decided by law. Thirdly, no merely abstract *right* should be granted to any class in the community, until they have attained the *might*, *i.e.*, the moral and intellectual power fitting them to exercise it. This is especially true in old countries, where, even under the most despotie forms, a working balance among the different parts of the State somehow succeeds in getting itself established. The reactionary excesses of the French Republicans at the time of the Revolution, were the best refutation of their principles. Universal suffrage, established on merely theoretical grounds, is impolitic. The fallacy lies in applying the principles of Social-morality to class interests —a capital error. In any complication Class-morality will be applied, not the Social-morality which the theorists expect. The appeal will not be to Reason, but to Interest. To believe that where power exists, it will not in time be exercised, is simplicity. There have been many extensions of popular privilege since the days of Elizabeth, but the prerogatives of the Crown have departed. Who does not see that the one is the inevitable consequence of the other? And lastly, I conclude that in the world, and among the relations of men, there is no such thing as Abstract Right, but only in God and the Human Soul; and that the only practical measure of Right is Might, or the power of using means to ends. But to return.

As Might plays the *active* part in the balancing of external conditions, so the power of Adaptation plays the *passive* part. The balance that is everywhere kept between animals and their habitats and supply of food, between all organisms and their environment, is secured by this power. Mr. Darwin's book on the 'Origin of Species,' and indeed the whole philosophy of Evolution is simply a detailed illustration of this fact. I have shown above that the radical Tendencies of all creatures are fixed and unaccountable. Their organisations, however, are changeable and modifiable by surrounding conditions. In man, speaking broadly, the Intuitions are the *fixed* Tendencies, the Understanding is the *adapting* power.

We have seen, then, that the World is constituted of a series of balances, on an ascending scale. In physics, we found that action and reaction were equal, that there was an equilibrium in ebb and flow, centripetal and centrifugal motions, in the compensating alternations of day and night, sleep and wake. We found that 'all mental action consisted of differentiations and integrations of states of consciousness,' that the balance between these two opposite states is necessary to health, insanity being nothing but fixedness of thought without change, or incessant change without rest. We have seen, too, that the perturbations of the passions in nations or individuals, were balanced by natural reactions ; 'swarmeries.' of opinion, by insight ; and local idolatries, by change of association. In the domain of Science we saw that the immense variety of scientific facts was balanced by the laws that underlie them,—individual facts, by generalisations, and the widest generalisations, by unity. Rising still higher into the region of the Intuitions, we found that the moral sentiment was the balance to selfishness ; the *public* nature in us to our *private* interests ; benevolence to helplessness, and hope to fear. And further, in looking at the conversion of truth into action, we saw the same provision made. We found that the dangerous nature of the elements was counteracted by science and art ; that Custom balanced Innovation ; the Conservation of the Good, perpetual Change ; Conservatism, Reform ; might, the resistance of circumstances ; and the power of adaptation, the changes of the environment.

Such being the Constitution of the World, I wish now to point out the Unity of Plan running through the whole, so that begin where you will, you find the same principle at work. Take, for instance, our progress in culture. We observe a few facts, and throw them into a general principle of belief. On this, we stand and act, while acquiring further experience. We then enlarge our first principle to balance the increase of facts, throw the whole into a general principle again, and so on, throughout the whole of our education, which is only a repetition of the same process carried upwards to higher and higher planes. The progress of society is the same. Certain ideas are in the air and dominate an age, balancing its acquired experience. These determine the form of government, and on these it stands and works. Succeeding generations, with wider knowledge and increased power, finding themselves cramped by the institutions of other days, either slowly stretch or violently rupture the bands, and throw out institutions more in accord with present needs. This process repeats. itself, through the successive stages of Despotism, Monarchy, and Democracy. In religion, too, the same process is seen in the progress from Fetishism and Man-worship, up to the most refined forms of transcendental Theism.

Again, if we take a general survey of the World, we shall see that this Unity of plan is not fanciful or theoretical, but is worked into the very texture of things. Take, for instance, the balance that is everywhere kept between *public* and *private* interests. No leaf is suffered to overshadow the plant, but in form and proportion is chastened into harmony with the whole. Goethe said that provision was made that no tree should grow into the sky. Vegetable and animal life are so balanced, as to keep the proportion of gases in the atmosphere constant. An animal is furnished with powers of aggression and self-defence, but subserves the harmony of the whole by being the prey of another. In man, the nature of this *public* element is found to be Moral. The Moral Sentiment in us compels us to respect the general good, while pushing our individuality and self-interest to the farthest point.

We have seen, then, that the world is an ascending scale of balances, with Physical forces at the bottom, Moral at the top ; a ladder with its foot on Earth, its summit in Heaven. We have seen, too, the unity of plan running through the whole system of things to the remotest fibre ; so that the most insignificant object, even a grain of sand or blade of grass, is a microcosm, or mirror of the Universe.

And now we have to determine whether the Cause of all this is Physical or Moral, *i.e.*, whether the Physical forces at the bottom are the same that appear (under other names) at the top ; or whether the Moral Power, that is consciously present at the top, is the Soul and animating principle of the whole.   A little reflection will show it is the latter. One secret of the world is, that although the evidence of Power is everywhere manifest, the *character* of that Power only appears in the highest organizations.   Let me illustrate this.   There is a gradation of rank in the vegetable and animal kingdoms, ascent on ascent of organization and powers. But nowhere, except in the human mind, is this Scale present as a *conscious* intuition.   The unceasing struggle of Nature to pass into higher forms (as it has done in the past), and to attain a purer expression, becomes in Man a *conscious* impulse. The same is true of Beauty.   The order of the world is maintained by a system of balances.   The perfection and harmonious play of these balances is beauty.   It is this harmony that constitutes the beauty of leaf and flower, plant and tree, animal and man, of feature and character, of music, dancing, poetry, and art.   I doubt not it was in this sense that Goethe said, 'The Beautiful includes in it the Good.'   But although beauty is everywhere present in Nature, in the Human Mind alone is it a *conscious* intuition.   Again, the adaptation of means to ends, known to us as intelligence, is seen everywhere.   Nature constructs an eye on the same principle as we construct a telescope.   We discover independently the laws of mechanism, and

use them for our own purposes, and afterwards find
that we have been following the Divine Methods.
So, too, the Identity that underlies a variety of
forms, in Man becomes a *conscious* perception. The
same feeling may be expressed in many unlike
ways—in word or deed, in expression of eye, into-
nation of voice, or gesture of body. Through the
countless unlike actions of every day, we detect the
same character. The genius of a nation is expressed alike in its history, its drama, its art, its
literature. This Identity appears in Nature under
the most opposite external appearances. The wing
of a bird answers to the fore-limb of a mammal ; the
cannon-bone of a horse, to the middle metacarpal
of the human hand ; and the bones in the skull of
a fish, to those in the skull of a man. Endless
changes of structure, like the variations of a well-
known air, are wrought on a simple type. The
affinities, too, that are *felt* in the mind, pervade
matter also, and appear in the attraction and repulsion of atoms, in the chemical affinities, in magnetism, and in sex. The identity of the individual
mind behind all the illusions by which it is fasci-
nated and detained, in its progress from youth to
age, gives the Idealist a hint of Absolute Reality,
and of the illusoriness of the external world.

Again, the Will. We are placed here on earth
in the midst of thick-streaming influences. We are
surrounded by physical and moral laws which hem

us in on all sides. These laws are incessant in their action—are immutable and inexorable. But their existence becomes apparent only when objects are brought within their range. Were there no bodies to fall, gravitation would not have been discovered. The laws of chemical combination would never have been known, could the elements not have been brought into proximity. Had men not been brought into mutual relationship, the moral law would have remained hidden. Now, we are conscious of the Will as that free power, by which we can either bring ourselves and the objects surrounding us into polarity with these laws, or remove ourselves from their range. We dip the waterwheel into the stream, to turn the machinery of our mills. We put water into a heated boiler, to get its force for locomotion. We put ourselves under the law of Conscience, and have God himself for our support. We withdraw from the Divine currents, and become shrunk and desiccated. This Will, then, which in us is a *conscious* power, is seen throughout Nature in the beautiful adaptation by which everything is placed where it is wanted ; and is as plainly at work behind ' natural selection ' as behind our simplest choice.

And now we may see why the Cause of the Universe is moral. Because, although it is *consciously* present only in the mind of Man, it appears everywhere in Nature in objects that have no Moral

·Sense. It is the *public element*, which we saw' not only in the Moral Sentiment in man, but in the provision that is made to keep every leaf, every plant, every tree, and every animal in strict subordination to the welfare of the Whole.

The necessity for a balance is so imminent, that provision is made for it everywhere. The mind is self-balancing, and throws out a weight wherever it is needed. Our desires stretch out to infinitude, but in this finite world full gratification is impossible. We contract our wishes, and so re-establish a working balance. The squalid ' houses of arrest' in Paris, in the Reign of Terror, were crowded ·with prisoners awaiting their fate. Under such circumstances, we might have expected the anxiety and tension of mind to have been extreme. But, by an inherent necessity, a reaction quickly followed, and they threw out surroundings that would balance their painful situation. They fell into ·order, took their respective ranks, started music ·and games, flirtatious and jealousies, and with ghastly mimicry ' acted the guillotine.' The literature of Europe from the fifth to the tenth century ·is a fine illustration of the same necessity. It consisted in little but legends of the saints and mar-.tyrs. In real life, physical force was the sole appeal in all disputes. There were no general principles ·of right, no high moral principles abroad, no power in moral force to shield from outrage. Chivalry had not yet appeared, slavery was everywhere prevalent, and in the world, the higher intuitions of the mind and the finer sensibilities of the heart were painfully denied their arena. And yet see how the mind was necessitated to throw out a balance. To have cut off the higher elements of our nature for want of a sphere of activity, would have been to dissipate the mind itself, and would have been as impossible as to find a positive without a negative pole to a battery. These legends were adapted to the particular strokes of Fate to which men were exposed. They turned on the cruelties of slavery and the blessings of liberty ; on the power of moral rather than of physical force ; on purity of feeling ; on affection and sympathy, kindness and sensibility.

The same necessity gives rise to the whole em pire of *illusions*. The boy requires surroundings that will give his nature a firmer poise than his schoolbooks can afford. He throws them out in his amusements and games, which have all the force of reality with him, and with which he is thoroughly in earnest ; while the girl takes naturally to dolls. Later, as his mind develops, he requires a more delicate and elevated thought on which to rest, and he surrounds his early love with the flower of his fancies. This is a beautiful and glorious unfolding, and communicates an infinite elasticity to the whole nature. In adult life we require a hero to satisfy our longing for harmony, and as an offset to the prosy monotony of the world. If we cannot find a real, we make an artificial one, and agree that he shall represent and embody our thought. The jury is packed, and we give him every allowance. For a time his autho rity is final. Agreement with his opinion, and approximation to his practice, become the measure of truth and beauty, in thought and action ; while dissidence is the measure of deformity. Late or never we find his limitations, and learn that our ideal exists in God alone.

The same necessity is the origin of all religion, poetry, and art. The tardy world comes late to its maturity, but in the meantime we anticipate the dilatory fact, by constructing for ourselves an ideal world. Religion is the auxiliary on which we rely to counteract the powers of Necessity, and as we have seen, its character is the reflection of our culture.

'Poetry,' says Carlyle, ' is the attempt man makes to render his life harmonious.' Beauty is everywhere present in the World, but has not as yet freed itself from the impurities of organisation. It is diffused through matter, like a delicate aroma, and requires fine sensibilities for its detection. The poet traces the finer lines that escape the common eye. As the diffused electricity of the atmosphere can be collected by art, and condensed into Leyden jars ; so, in the poem which the true poet gives us, we have the condensed beauty of the World. In music, too, there is something that cannot be found in life. Jean Paul Richter says of it, 'Away! away! thou speakest to me of such things as in all this endless life I have not found, and shall not find.' The necessity of a balance makes the fasci nation of art, and is shown in all degrees of pro ficiency, from the rudest scrawlings of the child to the beautiful idealisations of Raphael and Angelo.

And now, in concluding, I have to point out that, besides the successive planes of equilibrated thought, there is also, in the World and in the Human Mind, *the Divine*. This is the deep back ground, the mysterious incomprehensible Life that envelops us all ; the Spirit, from which emanate the countless myriads of creatures that bloom their little lives and fade away ; out of which we have emerged for a moment, and into which we vanish ; a thing of wonder, unspeakable, awful. Over its unfathomable depths, the endless procession of life glides like ripples over the deep sea. It is the endless generator of things, the source of this per petual *becoming*. It is the *Public Nature* of the World, and is seen less in individual objects, than in the landscape ; in individual actions, than in moral order ; in special talents, than in genius. As it is in the World, so it is in the Human Mind. It is this, which we feel to be the real balance power in the constitution. It is this that gives Truth its power, Virtue its courage, Love its sacrifice, but is itself no special point of truth, virtue, and love. It is this to which all men appeal for justice from oppression. It is this that shines through all the fetishes, images, or deities, under which, in different ages and stages of culture, men have sought to embody the Divine Idea. It is this to which all men draw nigh to worship. It is this which is the infinite horizon of truth, which we for ever approach and which for ever recedes. It is this which inspires virtue, but before which each particular virtue fades, and which lures us on to higher efforts. It is this which inspires success, and then condemns it in the light of more glorious attempts. We cannot define it or comprehend it, but ' it exists, and will exist.' To this Being we have given the name of God.

GOD OR FORCE ?

IN the minds of many cultivated people, at the present time, there is a growing belief in the efficacy of Science to solve the deepest problems of life. There is an increasing tendency towards scientific teaching in our schools and colleges ; and books are written to show, that of all kinds of education, it is of the most value, morally and intellectually. Students leave the lecture-room imbued with its principles, and its methods are believed to be of universal application to the affairs of life. Ever and anon, the world is apprised of some new discovery, which threatens the existence of consecrated dogma or traditional belief. Its facts have accumulated from year to year, and its present large body of systematised knowledge, has seemed to its leaders sufficient to justify some attempt at a theory of the Universe. Mr. Herbert Spencer has undertaken the task, and has worked it out elaborately in his Philosophy of Evolution. This philosophy rests entirely on scientific inductions, and, proceeding from generalisation to generalisation, ever widening and deepening, at last brings us

down to an *Unknown Force* as the Cause of all
things. An Unknown Force our God! and, in an
age, too, when all our old beliefs have fallen into
decrepitude. The effect of this last result of
scientific thought on the present age, may be easily
foreseen. Not a few will have already felt its
blighting influence on their lives and character.
Many who have the heart and capacity to worship,
will attempt in vain to kneel before this cold abstraction, and, in despair, will fly back to their
early creed. The more narrow, intense, and egoistic
minds will become its undisguised propagandists,
and boldly avow their atheism. Some will plod on
in sluggish discontent, or plunge into excesses;
while the excitements of wealth and ambition will
afford to others a passing solacement. But to a
few life would be unendurable without belief in a
God. These will press on, through thickening
doubts, to the very midnight of unbelief, lonely
and hopeless, surely, but still onward, till they
either fall weary by the way, or cheered by glimpses
of the approaching dawn, gather new courage and
come out into the freshness of morning and the
glorious sun once more.

The present writer has had his own difficulty,
in lifting himself out of this fog of unbelief, into a
clearer atmosphere. He remembers well the long
misery he endured, after his first patient study of
Mr. Spencer's writings. Here was a theory of the

Universe, founded on an enormous mass of scientific
facts, of all degrees of certainty, clearly wrought out,
logically consistent, and cohering well in all its
parts, with evidences of candour, patient investigation, and great range and subtlety of thought,
visible on every page. No desire to blink difficulties or suppress obnoxious facts anywhere appeared, and over the whole rested a certain
philosophical calmness, which, by inspiring confidence, tended to conviction ; certainly the deepest
and most subtle system of Materialism of modern
times. The study of these writings produced a
belief in the general conclusion there wrought out
—an Unknown Force at the bottom of all things,
which you clearly perceived was no God, although
you were invited to satisfy your religious feelings
at that altar. With nothing to fill up the heart,
the result was naturally a weariness of life, which
(in the absence of the usual objects of ambition,
which were felt to be illusions that could not
satisfy any deep spiritual longing), was now without an aim. The routine actions of every day, not
being quickened by life from above, or irradiated
by Duty (which had now become an empty name),
oppressed the spirit still more, and the sickened
heart turned from them with loathing. It seemed
as if there were to be no end to this state of mind.
I applied for assistance to one of our greatest
living thinkers, as I had inferred from his writings

that he had undergone a similar experience. He
gave me generous assurances of his sympathy, told
me not to despair, and that time would do everything for me. With lightened heart, I struggled on,
and the many inconsistencies which, superficially
seen, life presents, and which lend ready support to
atheism, were gradually lessened by more patient
study. This encouraged me to persevere until I
should arrive at such a harmonious view of the
World, as would satisfy my deepest feelings. The
remaining difficulties, one by one, gradually disappeared; and I now feel that no Materialism can
again shake the firm belief I have in a God who
made and still directs this Universe. The present
essay has been written with the desire of separating,
as far as possible, the larger threads, from the web
of thoughts and feelings that have influenced me in
this belief, for the consideration of those who can
find no rest for their souls in Materialism, but who
have, as yet, found no escape from its arguments
and conclusions. I shall aim only at presenting
the *leading* thoughts ; for all deep beliefs contain
elements so fine and evanescent, although none the
less influential, that it is impossible to reproduce
them all. The attempt will be facilitated, perhaps,
by a brief consideration of some of the leading
causes in philosophy and life, which have pre-
vented a harmonious view of the World. These
may be arranged under four heads :—

1. The neglect of the Scale in the Mind.

2. The attempt to account for the World from *without*, instead of from *within*.

3. The confusion in the choice of the instruments by which Truth is apprehended.

4. The looking at the World with too microscopic an eye.

The Scale in the Mind.—This is the deepest fact in the human consciousness, standing at the back of all our thoughts, feelings, and impulses, and giving them their relative dignities. It will be best described, perhaps, by indicating the part it plays in our intelligence, which is built up and organised around it, like crystals. The havoc that would be made of all our ideas, if it were cut out of the mind, attests its importance. Properly speaking, it is not a faculty, but is rather the *measure* of the faculties, giving them their relative subordinations. By it Justice, Goodness, Truth, and Beauty are marked *high*, while the physical sensations, appetites, and passions are marked *low*. All persons and institutions take their ranking from it, and the hierarchy in the world and in society is but a better or worse reflection of this hierarchy in the mind ; and without it would fall into chaos. It is, perhaps, the most important distinction, too, between Man and the lower creation. Animals have no scale. With them, nothing is either high or low, noble or base. They follow

all their instincts indifferently, without compunc-
tion and without choice. The Scale is the same in
all men, and has preserved its immutability through
all ages. The Feejean, it is true, considers murder
a high and noble act, while we consider it a base
and execrable one. But it is not the Scale that
has varied. It is merely a difference of opinion
as to *what* actions are to be ranked high and what
low, such as we find in a greater or less degree in
every age and nation. By the Scale, too, we get the
idea of *quality* as distinguished from *quantity*.
Hence a spark of high virtue outweighs mountains
of utility. The materialists attempt to show that
unselfishness springs from selfishness, that reverence and conscience spring from fear, and that
beauty springs from an aggregate of low, pleasur-
able associations. But these respective attributes,
as they range themselves along the Scale, are seen
to be as different in their essential natures as a
beautiful flower is different from the unsightly root
out of which it grows. It is the Scale alone that
puts the immense interval between force of Mind
and force of Gravitation ; and, without it, God and
Force were one. It for ever repudiates the boasted
victory of Science over Religion, by announcing
that the essential truths of each lie on different
planes. By it we are forced to believe that the
First Cause of things is not only more powerful,
but also *higher* than ourselves. By it we are made

to feel that Pleasure is only a *means*, but that ele-vation in the scale of Being is the *end* of human existence. It has been remarked by Carlyle that there is nothing so interesting to Man as Man, as is proved by the large element of personality that enters into nearly all conversation. I might add that in conversation respecting persons, there is nothing so interesting as this ranking of men and their procedure, as good, bad, indifferent, and the like. The greater number of adjectives, perhaps, in every language reflect in one form or another the Scale in the mind. They express different shades of quality and attribute, in positive, com-parative, and superlative degrees.

From the above considerations it is evident that the Scale plays so important a part in the Mind, that any philosophy which ignores or neglects it is doomed. Its neglect was the root-error in many of the ancient philosophies. The Epicureans, for example, made Pleasure the end of life. Under the one term they mixed and confounded the pleasures of virtue and the pleasures of sense, and gave the preference to bulk rather than to quality—to the sand and gravel rather than to the precious stones. If the pleasure that Socrates felt in rubbing his leg after his fetters were removed was greater than the sublime blessedness he felt in dying for virtue, it was to be preferred and followed. They thus ig-nored the Scale entirely, and in doing so failed to see that between the higher and lower pleasures there can be no comparison made, as there is between them no community of nature or attribute. The Stoics, in their reaction against the Epicureans, fell into the same error under another form. They made Virtue the only good, and everything else indifferent, neither good nor evil. In doing so they lost sight of the graduation ; for, although Virtue is the highest good, many other things are good also, if in a less degree. Modern Scientific Materialism is convicted of inadequacy for the like reason. It professes to account for the phenomena of life, mental as well as physical, by physical laws alone, *i.e.*, by the knowledge which is derived through the outer senses. But to the senses there is no Scale. To the senses there can be no difference in dignity between the motions of the matter which forms a crystal, and the motions of the nervous fluid which forms a thought. To the senses, there can be no difference in nature between the motions of the brain which correspond to a feeling of magnanimity and self-sacrifice, and the motions which correspond to a feeling of self-love and selfishness. The Materialist, therefore, cannot assume the Scale. If he does assume it, it is only by abdicating his own standpoint, and working out his theories by the help of an intuition which he professes to discard. If he does not assume it, he is committed to endless absurdities. For without it he cannot show that man is superior to the vegetable ; that self-sacrifice is higher than selfishness ; duty, than dishonesty ; reverence, than fear. Mr. Spencer, the most wary and far-sighted of the Materialists, when he is consistent with himself, ignores the Scale, and we shall now see what it reduces him to. He gravely asks us to consider whether, after all, there is much to choose between the force of *mind* and the force of *heat*. Mind, he is willing to admit can do some things which heat cannot. For example, it can invent a sun-glass, and bring the rays of the sun to a focus. But heat, in other respects, has the advantage over mind, inasmuch as it can melt the diamond which is placed within that focus. This comes of ignoring the Scale. But when the absurdities to which his philosophy reduces him begin to thicken around him, he is forced illegitimately to assume the Scale. He then tells us that life is *high* in proportion to the complexity and extent of an animal's relations. For this reason a man is higher than a beaver, a beaver than a polyp. But, unless the Scale is assumed, why should the more complex organisation be *higher* than the simple ? Why not the simple be higher than the complex ? If he reply that the more complex can fulfil a greater number of ends than the simple, we have still to ask why that should constitute it a *higher* thing ; and, again, no answer can be given, except by assuming the Scale.

Indeed, except by assuming the Scale, it would be impossible to show the superiority of mind over the clod of matter on which we tread.

Again, as Materialism cannot *assume* the Scale, neither can it account for it. It may point out the relation that exists between the nervous structure of the brain and our thoughts and feelings. It may argue that difference in structure necessitates difference in function. But although, in this way, it may account for *differences* in our feelings, it is impossible to account for this fixed *ranking* of them. It cannot be accounted for on any Experience or Evolution-hypothesis. The intuitive thinkers who accept the whole human consciousness as their standpoint, can, of course, consistently assume the Scale. But nowhere, as far as I am aware, have they brought it into the foreground, and used it as a philosophical weapon.

I now proceed to the second great cause of one-sided and inharmonious thinking, viz., the attempt to account for the World from *without, i.e.,* from the outer senses, instead of from *within, i.e.,* from the inner consciousness.

The Scientific Materialists, as I have said, attempt to account for the World by physical laws alone—that is to say, by the laws generalised from observations made by the outer senses. I shall now endeavour to show the hopelessness of their undertaking. To commence with, there are certain

regions of knowledge which are quite inaccessible
to the senses, and therefore to Science. Take,
first, our knowledge of human character. I see,
for example, certain manifestations of the feeling
which is known to us as anger. These manifestations consist of tones, looks, and gestures, all of
which are *unlike* to the senses. They have nothing
in common, and cannot therefore be generalised, or
reduced to a single principle. But by referring
them to a feeling which I have within myself, I at
once understand them. In like manner, a man's
love or ambition, his virtue or vice, his genius or
aspirations, are quite beyond the reach of the
senses, and can be known only from *within.* But
this interpreting element of feeling which is within
us, is precisely what Science cannot assume, as it is
pledged to interpret from the senses alone. The
utmost that Science can possibly do is to show
how the structure and action of the brain, of which
thought and feeling are the outcome, follow from
physical laws. But what relation is there between
the structure and action of the brain, and the *nature*
of the thought and feeling? There is none whatever. A few cells and fibres more, make all the
difference, in the eyes of 'Science, between a monkey
and a civilised European. A few cells more!
What a revelation there may be in these few cells!
What a dominating thought they may give the
world! There is clearly no relation whatever

between these cells and the nature of the thought they carry.

The highest works of genius, too, depend on knowledge which comes from *within*. Is not Shakspeare's acknowledged intellectual superiority due principally to his intense power of realisation; or of being, for the moment, the character he is describing? Does not his fine tracing of passion, in all its fluctuations, depend on his realising the situation from *within*? In music, poetry, and painting, the great master gives us this inner truth, and impresses on his works the harmony of his own inner nature. Science follows slowly in his footsteps, and merely arranges and gives laws to what he has invented. In this way have been formed the laws of composition, laws of colouring, and the like. History, again, must be interpreted from *within*. For what can we know of its heroes and heroic deeds, unless we can grasp the *spirit* by which they were inspired, by the *spirit* within ourselves. Political sagacity, too, depends on the statesman's power of realising the complex feelings, prejudices, and interests of the different classes in a nation, with the view of determining the effect that any piece of legislation may have upon them.

The highest and most important part of human knowledge is thus derived from our *inner* nature, and is entirely inaccessible to Science. But the materialists repudiate the inner feelings altogether as an instrument of knowledge. Mr. Spencer thinks that they disturb the intellectual balance, and accordingly discards them. Let me therefore indicate, still farther, the important part they play in our intelligence. We have already seen that love only can detect love, anger detect anger, sentiment detect sentiment. We have seen, too, that insight is the power of *realising* the same feeling in ourselves, as is in the object which we wish to understand. But, besides this, the feelings help the memory. A strain of music, for example, will often recall a train of long-forgotten circumstances, by arousing the feelings with which they were associated. Unity of feeling makes the poem. Impression or feeling is one of the finest ingredients in sagacity. The physician's impressions, after long practice, give him a finer apprehension of disease than the catalogue of symptoms in the books. The knowledge we get from experience is a mixture of vivid and faint impressions, or feelings. The vivid ones remain as clear and sharply-defined opinions. The faint ones lie in an unformulated state in the background of the mind, and go to make up our intuitions. For this reason our first impressions of men are often the best. All intuitive sagacity springs from this background of indefinite impression. And, lastly, the feelings are the hints we have given us of Final Cause. Otherwise, why have the feelings at all? Why not go through our necessary actions automatically, like the heart, liver, stomach, and other organs of the body? The difference in the nature of our different feelings indicates where the emphasis of thought and action is to be laid. In the lower appetites, passions, and propensities, for example, the feeling is short, intense, and *low* in character, indicating to us that, although most indispensable, they are not to be dwelt upon. The nobler sentiments and aspirations of our nature are, on the contrary, equable, long-continued, and *high* in character, indicating that they are to be pursued as permanent ends. And thus we see again that Pleasure is only a *means*, but that elevation of Character is the *end* of life.

That the Materialists should reject the inner feelings as instruments of knowledge, need not surprise us when we consider the *mechanical* method by which they arrive at truth in general. Mr. Spencer has the honour of the discovery, and after using it himself, he confidently recommends it to us, as the key to every philosophical difficulty. His plan, in short, is ' to compare all opinions of the same genus ; to set aside as more or less discrediting each other those various special and concrete elements in which such opinions disagree ; to observe what remains after the discordant constituents are eliminated ; and to find for this remaining constituent that abstract expression which holds true throughout its divergent modifications.'

That is to say, you are to take the opinion of everyone you meet, on any given point, rub these opinions together, until the last trace of divergence is worn away, and the common element that remains is the truth. Now I had always thought that the highest intellect would reveal the *highest* truth, and that between the opinion of Plato and a cowherd, or of Shakspeare and one of his own clowns, there was about as much in common as between the opinion of a man and an ape. This jumbling of all opinions can give us only the tritest and *lowest* truth ; and, indeed, it remains with Mr. Spencer to show why the ape's opinion should not be included also, now that the wall which formerly separated man from the brute has been cunningly removed by Scientific Thinkers.

We have seen, then, that Scientific thinkers, by taking their stand on the Senses, are excluded from the highest and most important part of human knowledge. Taking their stand on a *part* of the mind, only a *part* of the phenomena of the World is open to their method of research. It is absurd, therefore, for them to hope to account for the World by physical laws ; for no manipulation of a part can account for the whole.

The impossibility of accounting for the World by any scientific hypothesis will be further manifested, if we give the facts a different arrangement. The World consists of an endless diversity of objects, — rocks, earth, crystals, plants, animals, and Man. These objects are made up of forces of every description, which, for convenience, we may include under the terms physical and spiritual. The *order* in which these forces are manifested to us is known as the physical and spiritual laws of the World. The physical are discovered by the outer senses. The spiritual lie beyond the reach of the outer senses, and are known only to the inner consciousness. For example, the tendency that all bodies have to fall to the ground, is manifested to the sense of sight, and is a *physical* Law. **The** tendency that all men have to increase their power and influence, is only known to the inner senses, if I may use the term, and is a *spiritual* Law. **We** have equal certainty of the existence of these laws. They are alike uniform in their action, and can be predicted with equal confidence. Exceptions **to** either are equally the results of other laws contravening them. But, although we have equal knowledge of physical and spiritual *laws*, we have **not** equal knowledge of physical and spiritual *forces*. I can know the laws of heat and electricity, which the physicist announces from behind his batteries and retorts; but what do I know of the forces called heat and electricity? I cannot know them, because I cannot realise them in myself. But the spiritual forces I do know, for I can realise them in myself. Justice, Beauty, Goodness, Aspiration, I directly know from my own consciousness. Consider, too, the biologist. Armed with scalpel and microscope, he lays bare the inmost structure of animals, and announces the hidden resemblances that exist under the diversity of external appearances. The little bird that sings so sweetly to me, he gives a name to, and refers it to this or that species or class. He calls this a *knowledge* of the bird ; but, at bottom, what do I really know of the bird, but as much only of its little joy or grief as I can interpret from within myself. Looked at with the eye of Science, therefore, the World can be neither known nor understood, and is nothing more than a dead catalogue of unknown and unmeaning forces, lying around us, without end, aim, or unity. But looked at with the inner or *spiritual* eye, these forces are seen to combine, and to work for ends which we can ourselves realise and understand. They are seen to work for Beauty, Goodness, Justice, and Truth. Then Nature becomes alive with thoughts, which are also thoughts of our own minds ; she is no longer foreign and unrelated, but draws us to her by a poetic sympathy. I shall endeavour, farther on, to show how the forces of the World work together for these great ends.

In the meantime, I proceed to the third great cause of inharmonious thinking, viz., the confusion in the choice of the instruments by which the different orders of truth are to be apprehended.

Although the faculties of the mind, like the organs of the body, are mutually interdependent, and form an organic unity, like the organs of the body, too, they have each their own special and appropriate functions. The *senses*, for example, apprize us of the vicinity of objects that are to be sought or avoided—that are beneficial or injurious to us. The *generalising faculty* of the mind shows us the order and connexion of these objects, and shapes and adjusts them to our necessities and use. The inner *spiritual senses* find their sphere in the world of beauty, beneficence, and omnipresent Power around us, and pay homage to these in worship, art, and self-renunciation. The special senses cease their function when they have supplied us with the raw material of knowledge ; the generalising faculty, when it has given order to this material ; to the inner spiritual senses alone, is the Soul, that works through and behind all things, disclosed. We have many hints given us that these different instruments of knowledge are limited in their range, and soon discover that any mistake in their application is punished by confusion of thought. The eyes are adapted only to a limited range of vision ; the touch to a limited degree of fineness. When the mind (basing its judgments on experience) passes the finite, it becomes self-contradictory, and can neither conceive of space without end, nor of an end to space. The beauty that is apparent to the naked eye vanishes under the microscope, and the landscape pleases only when seen from a distance, where ugly details are lost to view.

Now, one of the most fruitful sources of error and confusion has been the presenting of spiritual truth in such a form as to subject it to the tests of ordinary experience. It has been the bane of Religion, and one of the prime causes of atheism. Religion is the belief which is engendered in the soul of Man by the contemplation of the phenomena of the World. It refers not to visible Nature, but to that which lies *behind* visible Nature ; not to the moving phenomena of Time, but to their ever-present Cause. The knowledge of this ever-present Cause, like the knowledge of a man's mind or character, lies quite beyond the reach of the outer senses, and can be apprehended only by our inner spiritual nature. It is a formless belief in a formless Reality. It has nothing in common with the knowledge derived from experience. In thinking of a generalisation of Science, for example, we have always present to the mind the *image* of one or more of the facts or experiments from which it is deduced. But in thinking of the invisible Cause that lies behind Nature, we can have no such image. It is clear, therefore, that spiritual and religious beliefs cannot be tested in the same way, or brought before the same tribunal,

as beliefs founded on visible and sensible experiences. But we are so constituted that we can
only express our beliefs by symbols that are palpable to one or other of the senses. To commu-
nicate our thoughts to others, we embody them in
language. If they are poetic thoughts, they are
embodied in the language of metaphor, or in the
language of painting and sculpture. If they are
spiritual thoughts, they are embodied in creeds,
formulas, rituals, images, and the like. But as the
same thought may be expressed in a hundred
unlike forms, as the same poetic feeling may clothe
itself in a hundred different metaphors, as the same
trait of mind or character may be embodied in a
hundred different deeds, so the same spiritual conceptions may be represented by a hundred differ
ent symbols. It is true that one mode of ex
pressing a thought may, by its pertinency, be more
felicitous than another. It is equally true that
one spiritual symbol, by its harmony with our
knowledge and culture, and its power of calling up
the religious sentiment, may be more appropriate
than another. In so far as this is the case, it has,
of course, a greater relative value. But the best
symbol is, after all, only a symbol, and must not
be confounded with the conception which it exists
to represent. We never lose sight of this distinc
tion in works of art. We do not ask the artist to
give us literal truth in his picture of the landscape.

We are satisfied if, by the skilful disposition and combination of colour and form, he gives us the spirit of the scene. We do not ask the dramatist to give us literal truth in his dialogue. It is enough if he can make his fictitious characters so speak and act as to lay bare the secret springs and mo tives of the human heart. But we imagine that creeds and other spiritual symbols are, in them selves, fixed, unalterable, and essential truths. We have accordingly exacted as implicit a belief in them as in the spiritual truths which they symbolise. We have embodied our conception of God in a concrete form, and have exacted belief in that form. We have wrapped our spiritual conceptions in creeds, more or less sensuous and personal in character, and have exacted belief in those creeds. In thus binding *essence* and *form* into one concrete whole, we have brought it, like other concrete realities, to the tribunal of experience, and have subjected it to the criticisms of Science. This fatal error has been sternly compensated, as all error is. Science boasts of having hunted the Deity from covert to covert, pulling down His retreats, thin ning His adherents, until it is now believed He is a phantasy, and sceptics ask sneeringly, Where is your God? Creeds which were once fresh and young, when pressed, in their withered old age, on the lusty intellect of the nineteenth century, excite only aversion and disgust, and are ignominiously spurned. And thus Religion itself is insulted and degraded. There is scarcely a single high truth of the intuition which we have not dragged down and arraigned before the bar of experience. All attempts to obtain a favourable verdict from this tribunal have been ineffectual. The subtleties of the Schoolmen were barren of fruit. They discovered nothing, and established nothing, but ran round in an eternal circle. The endless iteration only weakened truth, and wore off its edge. The belief in the Immortality of the Soul, with all high thinkers, rests rather on a broad *intuition* than on a *catalogue of reasons.* But when the theologians got it on their anvil, they drew it out into a score of logical threads, which were snipped by the scissors of the materialists as fast as they were formed. The Trinity, too, when regarded spiritually as the expression of the relation existing between the Divine Cause and the sides of the human spirit, is a high and noble truth. But the *doctrine* of the Trinity, which originated in the desire to adapt this truth to the vulgar mind, and which was enforced by arguments drawn from the flame of a candle, was broken, when it had hardened into an article of faith by the same hammers which had forged it. Such. have been, and ever will be, the consequences of bringing down the high truths of our spiritual nature to the vulgar

platform of the senses, to be wrangled over by an
insolent and contemptuous logic. The cause of
this degradation of Religion lies in the imbecility of
the masses of men, and their inability to distinguish between *form* and *essence*. Kings, for example,
in the eyes of men of insight, exist merely as the
representatives of law, order, and justice. But
what do the masses know or care about the representative character of kings? They believe, on
the contrary, that they are there on their own
account, and by their own right, that they are of
different flesh and blood, and are as much an ordi-
nance of Nature as the sun and moon. In like
manner, creeds have to the wise only a representative or symbolical value. But to the vulgar, they
are part of the eternal decrees. Religious teachers,
unable to lift this dead weight of stupidity and
superstition, have sunk down to it and become part
of it. In so doing, they have brought on themselves the criticisms of Science, and have been
accessory to that scepticism which they so much
deplore.

The secret of harmonious insight lies in knowing, as Bacon says, when to contract the sight and
when to dilate it. To discover the physical and
organic laws of Nature, the naked senses alone do
not suffice. We have to arm them with instruments, which, like the microscope, increase their
power and delicacy. But we must drop these in-

struments when we come to investigate the broad relations that exist between one object and another, or between the different parts of the same object. The function of the biceps muscle, for example, is as clearly to flex the forearm, as the function of the eye is to enable us to see. But it is evident that if we were to decompose the muscle into the innumerable cells and fibres which go to form it, and apply the microscope to each of them in turn, we never could understand its function at all. In the same way, to see the harmony of the World as a whole, we must take the higher faculties as our point of interpretation. While, in Science, we take our stand on the outer senses, and use the microscope as an instrument of research, in World-insight we take our stand on the spiritual powers, and use the outer senses as instruments of research. Science, by itself, can never see the harmony or unity of the World. Its generalisations are based on a *likeness* which is palpable to the senses. But the World is made up of phenomena between many of which there is no such likeness ; as, for example, between a strain of music, a beautiful flower, and a poem. It is only when we take our stand on the higher faculties, that the subtle spiritual affinities, which unite these unlike phenomena, become apparent. The perception of these affinities gave Bacon that breadth and vastness of understanding for which he is so justly renowned. For analogy, which is the weakest and least significant of logical or scientific relations, is the most powerful of spiritual ones. There is variety at the circumference of the World, unity at the centre. To the outer senses all things are more or less unlike, less so to the generalising faculty, which shows laws running through them, until to the inner spiritual senses there is unity or sameness of impression. The truth is, insight into the World is got in much the same way as insight into the mind and character of Man. For how could I understand a man's mind or character except by the reaction his words and deeds have on my own mind? Or, indeed, how could I know that he had what we call a mind at all, except in the same way? His conscious soul cannot be seen, or in any way be made palpable to my senses, and yet it can be so manifested to me as to compel my belief in it. The belief in God comes in the same way, by the reaction of Nature on the mind. As the physical man is the mask that hides and yet reveals his spirit, so does Nature hide, yet reveal, God. The impression that Nature makes on the mind has the *highest* reaction on the Scale within us. What more could a visible, palpable God have? Scepticism can begin only when God is embodied in a material and sensuous form, and degraded. Otherwise there is no room for Atheism.

The fourth cause (and last that I shall mention

here) of inharmonious views of the World, is the looking at it with too *microscopic* an eye.

The doctrine of Divine Providence has been denied. Nature is seen to treat her children roughly, paying little regard to individuals. Disease and death are no respecters of persons. The laws of Nature, to which God is supposed to have committed the care of the Universe, are inexorable. But Providence is the connecting of the individual with the will of God. Some of the links in the chain appear to be wanting, and the individual is believed to be isolated from God. The links are not wanting, but are unseen. They cannot be traced to the individual, but become apparent when we look over large areas. The exquisite adaptation of every organism to its environment, is Providence. Even the mechanism by which I swallow my food, without being choked by it, is Providence. The minute arteries which supply every cell, in every organ of the body, cannot be seen. They are there, notwithstanding, as is evidenced by the continued vitality of the parts which they supply. If the oversight of the whole world is providential, it must be so of the parts also. If the world is advancing to any goal, it must be by the co-operation of the individuals in it. The men of this generation carry forward the ark of God to the point where it is taken up by the men of the next. Must not each of us, then, have his appointed lot? The

parent, losing his child by early death, asks, doubt-
ingly, if there can be a Providence, else why this
early bereavement.   He does not perceive that one
object of Nature's profusion is to provide against
the ravages of Necessity.   The oak produces thousands of acorns, the tree thousands of blossoms,.
for one that reaches maturity ; animals breed in
proportion to the dangers to which they are exposed ; but there is always enough for the purposes
of continuance and progression.   Again, it is asked,.
how account for Evil.   I see no evil in the *ground-
plan* of Nature.   As they exist in the Eternal Mind,
the threads of this web of physical, organic, and
spiritual forces, which constitute the World, are all
good ; but when Time commences, and the web is
being woven, their friction and interaction (which
we call Necessity) produce Evil, and in moral
natures, like Man, their opposition, unless chastened
into harmony, produces Sin.   But just as cold,
which seems to the senses to be a positive quality,
is really a negative, being the absence of heat, so
evil is positive to our moral nature, but to the
intellect has no existence.   And yet this Necessity
which is felt by the individual as evil, works out
good for the world, and is one of the main sources
of progress.

Having noticed a few of the leading causes that
have led to error and confusion in thinking, I shall
now endeavour to show that the forces of the World

work together for Character—or, in other words, for Justice, Beauty, Goodness, and Truth.

The World, as we have seen, is made up of physical, organic, and spiritual forces, and the problem of Philosophy is to find their connection and purport. Science deals with the physical and organic merely. These make up the structure of bodies. But *structure* is meaningless until *function* is interpreted. For example, digestion and assimilation are the functions of the stomach ; thought and character are the functions of the brain. It is evident that no scientific knowledge of the *structures* of these respective organs can enable us to understand the connexion and subordination of their *functions*. But by the knowledge derived from our own inner consciousness, we see at once their mutual relations. We see that digestion and assimilation exist as *means* for the support of bodily life, and that the support of bodily life is only a *means* to the higher ends of thought and character. Then, the end and purport of the structures themselves become manifest ; and, therefore, of the physical and organic forces of which they are composed. Take, again, the flower. To the eye of Science, it is only an aggregate of physical and organic forces ; but, to the inward eye, these forces are seen to be only the *means* for the production of that beauty in which they culminate. In the same way, the great World-forces that lie

around us are, to Science, only a meaningless
aggregate, without end, aim, or unity of purpose.
Mr. Spencer sees no difference between gravitation, heat, and mind. To him, they are merely
so many forces, differing in their manifestations,
but equal in dignity and power ; alike independent
and unrelated ; existing on their own account,
without hierarchy or subordination. How then do
we find their meaning ? Man is the epitome of
the World. All its forces are gathered into his
mind and body, and there receive their interpretation. The mechanical forces appear in the struc
ture of the heart, and the circulation of the blood ;
the chemical forces in the disintegration of the
food by the forces of the stomach, and its com-
bustion in the body ; the organic forces in the
secreting organs, and in the waste and repair of
tissues ; the spiritual forces in the mind. The fact
that the functions performed by the physical and
organic forces are unconscious and unobtrusive,
proves that they are only subordinate instruments,
and that Science, which deals with them, is only
an *instrument of investigation*, not a *standpoint for
interpretation.* The heart, lungs, and stomach, in
their healthy state, give us no intimation of their
existence ; their action is attended by neither pleasure nor pain ; proving that they are the necessary,
but subordinate instruments of higher ends. In the
lower animals, Self-preservation and Reproduction

occupy the largest portion of conscious existence, and are accordingly the highest functions. In Man, they occupy but a comparatively small portion, and leave room for the play and expansion of intellect and character. Seeing, then, that the physical and organic forces are only means and instruments, we may, in endeavouring to show the ends to which the Tendencies of the World are working, practically leave them out of account, and consider only those tendencies which have emerged into consciousness.

The Tendencies to *Self-preservation and Reproduction* are the most immediate and pressing. They are ministered to, not only by the special senses, physical powers, and lower appetites, but by pride, envy, vanity, combativeness, and fear. They furnish the warp into which Time has to weave his most variegated colours. There must be this continuous web of existence, for the Eternal to work out His designs.

The Tendency to *Ascension* runs through all highly-organised beings. Everything looks upwards. With animals Might is the test of Right. Physical Power is their highest distinction. The strongest have the best chance to survive and propagate, and to them the females are most strongly attracted. Women love the heroic, strong, and wise; and Beauty, in the last analysis, is only Nature's representative of these high qualities, and always refers to *spiritual* attributes. This tendency of the race to ascend on the ground of sexual preferences is secured to the individual by his mental constitution. We are all led by *Imagination*, which invests its object with a kind of in finitude, and leads us on to emulation. The dullest are led by it. It is neither the gold itself, nor the mere satisfaction of his physical wants, that dazzles the miser's eye, but the undefined region of delight that is opened up to his imagination. This leading of the Imagination appears early in life. The boy sees all the world in his games and youthful contests, and works for the prize at the village school as if it were a kingdom. The enamoured youth sees the best of everything in his maiden. The man falls into *Hero-worship*. Our admiration is the thing we ourselves would wish to be, and to which we endeavour to elevate ourselves. What a man in his heart admires most, gives the clue to his character. His talents all minister to it, and around it all his thoughts and feelings revolve. *Ideals* are only another phase of this ascending tendency. They are made up of the complex web of experience and imagination, and are the stars by which we direct our course through life. They lie, like glittering points, on all sides of the horizon, and towards them the busy world of men are seen making their way. The part played by *Individualisation* in the upward movement is no less important. On the circumference of the World is the immense diversity of things, where the game seems to be, how to ring the greatest number of changes on a few fixed principles. These separate exist- ences reflect on each other their own special beauties, and multiply to infinity the objects of aspiration. The love of personality plays an im- portant part in our education. We digest our code of morals from it, and endeavour to embody in ourselves the special virtues which we admire in others. Hence the charm and stimulus of biography, history, and novels, compared with which all mere scholastic teaching, which does not sink into the character, is trivial and superficial.

But these ideals, when attained, do not fill up the heart. The boy outgrows his sports ; the youth, his maiden; the man, his idolatries. Wealth does not satisfy ; place and power, when attained, lose the vagueness and brilliancy which dazzled us and drew us on, and shrink into littleness. The sen- sualist's path leads to disgust. Special attainments and points of virtue, too, fail to satisfy, and we learn at last that there is no rest but in God. Thus these illusions instruct while they deceive. But unless the mind is quick and apprehensive, we do not run to the end of this chain of deceptions, and so stop short of the goal. As long as our minds rest on any of these proximate objects of pursuit, we cannot dedicate ourselves to God, for two op- posite infinites cannot possess the mind at once.

There is another factor in Ascension which is too important to be passed over without notice, viz., the *antagonism* of the higher and lower forces of Nature and Mind. For example, the obstinacy of earth, wood, iron, develop invention and mechanical skill; the necessities of life and the complexity of our surroundings call out all our resources; and the control of the passions, so necessary to social order, exercises and strengthens virtue.

The foregoing tendencies exist only in the mind, and if they rested there progress would cease. How, then, is the world benefited? Observe, first, as a connecting link, the Tendency to *Unity*. Give a man time, and his mind will become a unity, and everything he does will be significant. His actions will become one with his feelings, and his feelings one with his thought. This tendency to unity makes possible the realisation of our ideals. Without it, life would want definiteness of aim. It concentrates the powers of the mind for united effort, and counteracts that love of variety, which, if persistently indulged in, confuses thought, relaxes the character, and dissipates organised effort. To reach it is the unceasing endeavour of the mind.

Connected with this Tendency to Unity is the Tendency to *Embodiment*. The World itself is the embodiment of Spirit; language, facial and bodily expression, are the embodiments of thought and feeling, of which Literature and Art are the more permanent forms. Character is the embodiment within ourselves of Thought, slowly built up and consolidated. Action, too, is the embodiment of Thought. In the pursuit of ideals, we pave every step with work, with action, and thus the world is benefited, although the individual may be sacrificed.

This Tendency to Embodiment is further assisted by the Tendency to *Belief.* Without this tendency, action would be weak and nerveless, not strong and direct. The belief we have in the beneficence of Nature is very beautiful. We give ourselves calmly up to sleep, and rest without suspicion, expecting to awaken to renewed life. We trust ourselves to the elements, to our food, its safe passage into the stomach and subsequent changes in the blood, and conversion into strength and beauty. We trust to the continued beating of our hearts, and the continuance of life from moment to moment ; to our continued sanity, 'although the chaos of madness lies always near us. We trust to the rotation of seasons, crops, and verdure, although the earth's surface is only a beautiful skin, beneath which boils a cauldron of confused elements. We trust that a man's character is truly represented by his sensible motions, although his soul cannot be seen ; and to the immutability of

God and His laws, although He himself is hidden from us.

The Tendency to *Co-operation* redoubles the force both of Belief and Action, and still further assists in keeping the *visible* world following in the track of the *ideal.* We all need sympathy. The high thought would die out of us, did it not meet with recognition from our fellow-man. Society, accordingly, is the arena where our talents find room to expand. The bond of union is always a common sentiment or idea. Friendships are founded on identity of feeling. Associations of men have always some dominant thought, around which they unite. Institutions are the visible expressions of those thoughts. Church and Government correspond to the two most comprehensive divisions of human interest—the welfare of the soul and the welfare of the body. Society, by providing for the lawful exercise of all our impulses, diminishes the temptations to crime. If the passions are strong, you may marry ; if the desire for property is strong, you may work, not steal. Government takes retaliation out of our hands, and leaves no room for private revenge; and by affording protection to all, gives the higher faculties of our nature a chance to expand.

But how are the accomplished results of human thought and effort secured against Time and Change ? By the Tendency to the *Conservation of the Good.* Time swallows all things but the Good, which steadily works on, and accumulates from age to age. Custom is one element in this tendency. The world is the slave of custom. To the aspiring youth, Truth itself seems powerless against it. On our entrance into life we are dressed in certain customary modes of thought, feeling, and behaviour, and many of us wear the same livery all our lives. We take our creeds from our fathers, and our morals as well as fashions from Society, and applaud or condemn as it dictates. These things are in the air we breathe, and this atmospheric education influences our conduct more than any other. Conformity to custom meets with the world's applause, and in every drawing-room appears in the form of stock-sentiment. But custom subserves a good purpose. It is the break on the wheel of change. It follows thought, although at a great distance, and keeps institutions alive until the good that was once in them has departed and entered into other forms.

Observe, again, how the best modes of alleviating physical labour are transmitted from age to age. Manual labour is superseded by machinery, and inferior machines are laid aside only when better come into use. The accumulation of scientific facts, the increase both in the number and the delicacy of scientific instruments, enlarge our knowledge of the physical laws. This knowledge reacts, in turn, on the arts, and produces still further improvements. These results are the slow accumulations of the ages which they have survived. In like manner there is a tendency to preserve all good books and all good works of art. Homer and Raphael still live to instruct the youth of the present day. History preserves the memorable experiences of the world, and leaves its daily trivialities to be forgotten. And thus the essence of the past is distilled into the present.

But there are *false* as well as *true* Ideals. These false ideals get embodied, and have sometimes dominated whole ages, producing endless confusion; and the question is, what prevents the world's retrograding?

Consider, first, the Tendency to *Justice.* Intellect is the power of discerning the Tendencies of the World in their natural subordinations. The observance of these laws is enforced by Justice. All civil, moral, and social codes, are but better or worse reflections of this dominating tendency. Nature has at heart the coronation of Virtue, and takes a short cut to her end by making Might the test of Right. This is the tune the nations have marched to, and throughout all its variations (which we call history) the original air is heard. The individual, too, if he sinks his nobility of character, loses influence, becomes less in the scale of being, and must submit to superior domination.

Again, the Tendency to *Adaptation* puts a cushion between us and the rough corners of things that have been jostled from their places. It enables us to float, when otherwise we should sink. We gradually adapt ourselves to new climates, new countries, new manners, new morals, and new modes of thought ; and die when age makes us too rigid for new and wider conceptions. Then there is the Tendency to *Compassion*, which breaks the force of Fate to which we are all exposed, and cheers the heart for new endeavours. The sympathy of our fellow-men redoubles the strength of all our active powers, invigorates the will, and gives fresh courage to despair.

The foregoing tendencies all unite to keep the world following in the track of the great men who march in the van. And we have seen that these men, after passing through all proximate illusions, find their ideal in God, and their final rest in reliance on Him alone. This is the consummation of manhood. When attained, it expresses itself in Heroism, Worship, and Art, which are ends in themselves, and which correspond to the different sides of our nature, its tendency to *Action, Contemplation*, and *Beauty*.

All things in Nature struggle towards Beauty ; and deformity, like evil, is the result of Necessity, and does not lie in the essence of things. The artist strives to restore this ideal beauty on canvas or stone, and its pursuit is a source of pure enjoyment, when cultivated in a religious spirit.

Worship should be the flower of Culture, the harmonious outcome of all our feelings, chastened and refined, and not a daub. It should be in the grain, not a mere veneering, and is the expression of inward peace.

The history of the world abounds in examples of Heroism. These great souls, scattered through distant ages and nations, and quickened before their time, are the high-water marks of humanity, and announce what, one day, will be universal. They reached the point where the human melts into the divine.

THE END.

LONDON : PRINTED BY
SPOTTISWOODE AND CO., NEW-STREET SQUARE
AND PARLIAMENT STREET

CPSIA information can be obtained at www.ICGtesting.com
Printed in the USA
BVOW07s2015060715

407617BV00012B/105/P